RBG's
BRAVE & BRILLIANT
WOMEN

RBG's
BRAVE & BRILLIANT
WOMEN
33 JEWISH WOMEN
TO INSPIRE EVERYONE

BY NADINE EPSTEIN

INTRODUCTION AND SELECTION BY
RUTH BADER GINSBURG

DELACORTE PRESS

Text copyright © 2021 by Nadine Epstein
Introduction copyright © 2021 by Jane Ginsburg and Jim Ginsburg
Jacket art and interior illustrations copyright © 2021 by Bee Johnson

Visit us on the web! rhcbooks.com

Educators and librarians, for a variety of teaching tools,
visit us at RHTeachersLibrarians.com

Library of Congress Cataloging-in-Publication Data
Names: Epstein, Nadine, author. | Ginsburg, Ruth Bader. | Johnson, Bee, illustrator.
Title: RBG's brave & brilliant women : 33 Jewish women
to inspire everyone / by Nadine Epstein ; introduction and selection by
Ruth Bader Ginsburg; illustrated by Bee Johnson.
Other titles: RBG's brave and brilliant women
Description: New York : Delacorte Press, 2021. | Audience: Ages 10 up | Summary:
"A collection of biographies of Jewish female role models—selected in collaboration
with Ruth Bader Ginsburg and including an introduction written by the Supreme
Court justice"—Provided by publisher.
Identifiers: LCCN 2021019972 (print) | LCCN 2021019973 (ebook) |
ISBN 978-0-593-37718-5 (hardcover) | ISBN 978-0-593-37720-8 (trade) |
ISBN 978-0-593-37720-8 (ebook)
Subjects: LCSH: Jewish women—Biography.
Classification: LCC DS115.2 .E67 2021 (print) | LCC DS115.2 (ebook) |
DDC 920.72089/924—dc23

The text of this book is set in 11.5-point Horley Old Style.
Interior design by Michelle Cunningham

MANUFACTURED IN ITALY
10 9 8 7 6 5 4 3 2 1
First Edition

Random House Children's Books supports the First Amendment
and celebrates the right to read.

....

IN MEMORY OF
Ruth Bader Ginsburg (1933–2020)
Celia Bader (1902–1950)
Ruth Epstein (1925–2012)

....

Tzedek, Tzedek, Tirdof.
Justice, justice you shall pursue.
—DEUTERONOMY (16:20)

CONTENTS

PROLOGUE

Sitting in her Supreme Court chambers in 2019, Justice Ruth Bader Ginsburg and I had a conversation about why female role models are important to people of all ages, especially young people. She was particularly interested in Jewish role models because she was deeply Jewish and keenly felt the age-old connection between social justice and Jewish tradition. The humanity and bravery of Jewish women, she said, had always sustained and encouraged her when her spirits needed lifting. This book was born out of that conversation.

Together Justice Ginsburg and I drew up a list of some 150 women with indomitable energy who moved the world forward. It was no easy task to narrow that list down to those in this volume but we finally did. The women we chose lived in ancient times and in times nearer our own, in faraway lands and here in America, and they each had different talents and interests. Whether of Ashkenazi, Sephardi, or Middle Eastern Jewish descent or converts, they were guided or shaped by Jewish beliefs or values.

- Some were poor and self-taught; others were rich and were fortunate to receive a better education than most women of their era.
- Some had parents who understood and encouraged them; others had families who stood in their way.
- Some had brothers who received preferential treatment; others had no brothers and were expected to do whatever sons might have done.
- Some married and had children; others didn't, some by their own choice.
- Some had hard lives; others never personally suffered.
- Some lived to old age; others had lives tragically cut short by illness or accident, or were killed in the Holocaust. Many faced anti-Semitism as well as gender discrimination.
- Some never saw themselves as torchbearers for other women; others were very conscious that they were trailblazers. A few were proud to be called "troublemakers."

What they all have in common is that they transcended what was expected, allowed, or tolerated for a woman of their time. They chose difficult or unusual paths and stayed true to their talents and missions despite the obstacles. They achieved what was unimaginable, and the unimaginable led to the advancement of women, to breaking barriers in previously men-only fields, and to changing the world for the better.

However you read this book—from front to back, from back to front, or randomly dipping into the stories of these smart and strong women—you'll find at least a few women whose lives will inspire you to make a difference and maybe even to change the world!

When we began *RBG's Brave & Brilliant Women*, Justice Ginsburg was eighty-six, physically frail, and had already fought off cancer several times. Even when she learned it had returned, she kept working on this book, often sending me suggestions and edits faster than I could respond to them. She was determined that this book would be part of her legacy to you. This is but one example of how this strong-willed, forward-looking person never stopped fighting for what she believed in.

Justice Ginsburg died on September 18, 2020. The world lost a brave and brilliant woman, and I lost a friend.

In the Jewish world, when someone dies, it is customary to say Baruch dayan ha'emet, which means "Blessed be the true judge."

She was a true judge. So let us say, "Blessed be the true judge."

INTRODUCTION BY RBG

People often ask me about my role models. In my growing up years, the term *role model* was not yet coined. And it wasn't easy to learn about the many great women who had changed the world for the better—and paved the way for women like me to attend colleges and universities, and become lawyers, doctors, or violinists in orchestras. None of the women in the Book of Exodus—not even Miriam—were in the Haggadah used by my grandparents at family seders. The two biblical women young Jewish children knew about at the time were Ruth, who loyally followed her mother-in-law Naomi, became an Israelite, and eventually married a wealthy man, and Esther, who saved her people by being so beautiful that King Ahasuerus chose her in a competition to be his new No. 1 wife. In contrast, the Bible tells us many stories about men.

In the public library I visited weekly while my mother had her hair done, biographies of women were rare. It's still true today that men are more often the central character in storytelling books. That's why we want to tell you the stories of brave and brilliant Jewish women, women who didn't accept the tradition that a woman's only place is in the home, women who wouldn't settle for the rules prevailing in past generations and communities.

Looking back to my youth, I did know of and particularly admired two Jewish women, both raised in the United States of America, women whose humanity and bravery touched me deeply. One was Emma Lazarus, a poet most famous for writing "The New Colossus," the poem engraved on the base of the Statue of Liberty in New York Harbor. Her poem has welcomed millions of immigrants, including my father and grandparents—people who came to the United States to escape fear and persecution and longed for a safe and free place to live. Emma Lazarus's love for humankind, for America, and for the Jewish people, is evident in all her writings. Her first book of poetry was published in 1866 when she was seventeen. She wrote constantly until she died far too soon, at the age of thirty-eight.

The other woman who inspired me greatly was Henrietta Szold, who founded and ran Hadassah, an American Jewish volunteer women's organization launched in 1912, long before women were considered able to lead large organizations. Szold was born in 1860, eleven years after Emma Lazarus, and she lived until 1945. My mother spoke of Henrietta Szold glowingly. What did she tell me? Henrietta Szold was determined to create a homeland for the Jewish people even before Theodor Herzl and other men took on the Zionist cause. Among her many projects, Szold started night schools to teach English and trades skills to the waves of Jewish immigrants coming from Russia and other Eastern European countries in the late 1800s and early 1900s. My father, who was born in Russia, didn't speak English when he arrived in New York in 1909 at age thirteen. He was the beneficiary of a night school education of the kind started by Henrietta Szold.

I also knew of Deborah, the only female judge mentioned in the Bible, and one of only seven female prophets in the entire Jewish tradition. She was also a military leader. I am not a general or admiral, but like Deborah, I am a judge proud to be a Jew. She made her judgments beneath a date palm tree in ancient Israel and I have the good fortune to be a Justice on the Supreme Court of the United States, the country's highest court.

A woman's voice and a woman's experience have much to contribute to the art of judging. That's why we need more women judges—and more women on the Supreme Court. People sometimes ask me, "When will there be enough women on the Court?" I reply, "When there are nine." For centuries there were nine men and everyone thought that was completely normal. Why should it not be similarly normal to have a court of nine women?

We need not only more women judges. We need more women leaders in all fields. In this book you will find many extraordinary women you can admire, women who can inspire you to become whatever your talent permits you to be. I was fortunate enough to know some of the women in the book personally. Others I have only read about, but wish I could have met.

Once you choose your role models (it's good to have many!), I hope you set your mind to do great things and stay steady on your course. The world needs more brave and inspirational people. You can be one of them.

— Ruth Bader Ginsburg
WASHINGTON, DC, 2020

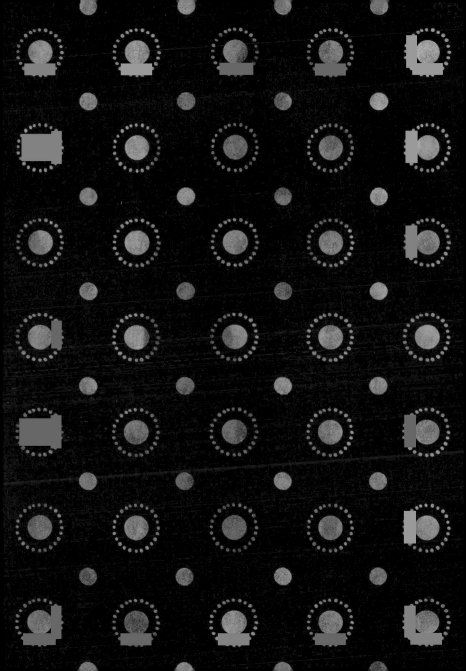

RUTH BADER GINSBURG

*Supreme Court Justice and
Role Model to a Nation*

*DID YOU KNOW THAT NOT ALL THAT LONG AGO GIRLS
WEREN'T PERMITTED TO STUDY THE SAME SUBJECTS
AS BOYS?* That there were hardly any sports teams for
girls, and girls weren't allowed to play on the boys'
teams? That it was nearly impossible for women to be
astronauts, firefighters, police officers, doctors, lawyers, or even bartenders? That married women didn't
have the right to own a house, open a bank account,
have a credit card in their own names, or have cus-
tody of their children if they were divorced? And that
until a little more than one hundred years ago, American women did not have the right to vote in presidential
elections?

Things are different now, and girls and women have
almost the same opportunities as boys and men—and
can achieve as much or even more than men they know if
they put in the hard work. But it took a long time and the

efforts of thousands of people, both women and men, to win these rights.

One of those people was Ruth Bader Ginsburg, who served on the U.S. Supreme Court in Washington, DC, the highest court in the United States, from 1993 until her death on September 18, 2020. Justice Ginsburg, who in her later years was so famous that people referred to her simply as RBG, made American law fairer, making an enormous difference in people's lives.

RBG was born in 1933 in Brooklyn. Her father, Nathan Bader, was a Jewish immigrant who had come to America from Odessa, a city in the Russian Empire. He was a furrier when he met his wife and Ruth's mother, Celia Amster Bader, a bookkeeper in New York's garment district. Celia was of Austrian Jewish descent and her parents were Orthodox Jews who followed the old traditions regarding sons and daughters. They used what little money they had to educate their son but not their daughter. Perhaps this is part of the reason that Celia Bader always encouraged young Ruth to do well in school, and taught her that she could do anything to which she set her mind. Ruth was especially close to her mother, and followed her advice.

"My mother told me two things constantly," RBG often said. "One was to be a lady," which meant conducting herself civilly and not letting emotions such as anger or envy get in her way. (Later RBG's mother-in-law added that a little "deafness" to thoughtless and unkind words is a wiser choice than reacting in anger or annoyance.) The other was to be independent and capable of earning her own living, which, as RBG once explained, "was an unusual message for mothers of that time to be giving to their daughters."

Ruth was an excellent student at the Brooklyn public schools she attended, and in 1946, her parents watched proudly as she gave the valedictory speech for her eighth-grade class. She also studied at the East Midwood Jewish Center, the Conservative synagogue to which her family belonged, where she learned about Jewish history, holidays, and ceremonies, and even mastered some Hebrew. Her congregation did not allow girls to become bat mitzvah, the equivalent of the bar mitzvah ceremony for boys, but she and the other girls in her class were confirmed in a group ceremony, also in 1946. She wrote two pieces in the synagogue bulletin's graduation issue that give us clues about what she was thinking about at the time. One was a tribute to a famous rabbi, Stephen S. Wise, whom she praised for his support of women's suffrage. The other was the lead article, in which she remembered the horrors to which the Jewish people were subjected in

Nazi death camps, and argued that "for righteous people, hate and prejudice are neither good occupations or fit companions." That summer, Ruth attended a Jewish camp in upstate New York, where she would later work as a camp counselor.

In high school, Ruth continued to be a stellar and popular student, but life wasn't easy for the Ginsburg family: Celia was diagnosed with cancer and underwent years of painful treatments. Then, the day before Ruth was to graduate from high school, Celia died. Ruth stayed home from graduation to mourn with her father. In observance of Jewish tradition, family and friends gathered at their home as Ruth and her father sat shiva. As is the custom during this seven-day mourning period, at least ten Jews, called a minyan, said prayers together for her mother. Ruth knew the prayers and wanted to participate, but she was excluded, because in those days women did not count as part of the minyan—and still do not today in most Orthodox circles.

"One of the searing memories of my youth was when my mother died and there was a minyan every day, and I couldn't be part of it," she once told me. "That really hurt me." This early encounter with gender discrimination led her to rebel against the traditional practice of Judaism, though she continued to be deeply inspired by

Jewish values and her Jewish identity remained important to her throughout her life.

Ruth graduated from college, married a fellow student, and went out into the world. There she experienced gender discrimination of a more practical nature.

She experienced it at her first job out of college when her boss took away her responsibilities when she told him she was pregnant.

She experienced it as one of only nine women in a class of 534 at Harvard Law School, where some male students and professors didn't think women could make good lawyers—and some of the buildings where classes were held didn't even have restrooms for women.

She experienced it when she graduated from Columbia Law School tied for first in her class: Although she was highly qualified and was interviewed at many law firms, not a single firm offered her a job.

She experienced it when she found a job as a law professor and was told her salary would be less than that of men who did the same work.

The lawyer who would become the second woman appointed to the Supreme Court was even rejected from a Supreme Court clerkship because she wasn't a man!

RBG persevered. Her personal experiences and the discrimination she saw all around her propelled her toward a legal career fighting on behalf of the rights of American girls and women, and others who were denied rights they deserve.

From a lawyer's point of view, the problem was that the men who wrote the U.S. Constitution in the 1700s never mentioned women in it and American law is based on the Constitution. The first time women's rights were addressed was in 1920, when the Nineteenth Amendment declaring that the right to vote shall not be denied on account of sex was added to the Constitution. This was a huge step forward, but federal and state legislatures and the courts did not interpret the new amendment in ways that would have opened the doors to equal rights and opportunities for women in other areas. As a result, when RBG was born in 1939, women could still legally be prohibited from working in certain jobs—and even could be prevented from serving on juries. They could vote, but they remained second-class citizens.

As a young lawyer, RBG sought to find a way to expand the rights of women and to enshrine them in American law. First she founded and led the pioneering Women's Rights Project at the American Civil Liberties Union (ACLU). Then she carefully chose cases that challenged laws that required men and women to be treated differently in the same situation and argued them before the Supreme Court. Cleverly, she selected laws that appeared to favor women over men, including one that allowed a woman whose husband had died to receive government benefits to stay home with her children, but refused the same benefits to a man whose wife had died.

RBG argued that women were covered under the Equal Protection Clause of the Fourteenth Amendment, which was added to the Constitution in 1868, three years after the Civil War ended, and required every state to provide equal protection under the law to all people. Using this approach, she won five out of six cases she argued before the Supreme Court, and so, in the 1970s, more than fifty years after American women won the right to vote, she found a way to demonstrate that women had equal rights under American law. Basing women's rights on an old amendment originally meant to cover newly freed slaves wasn't a perfect solution, but the effect was that it finally became illegal to treat women as separate or subordinate to men. At that moment, U.S. law became fairer not just for women but for men and families as well. RBG's achievement was especially important since around the same time, a proposed amendment that specifically called for equal rights for women—the Equal Rights Amendment—wasn't approved by enough states and so did *not* become part of the Constitution.

RBG's feat did not go unnoticed. In 1980, she was appointed as a judge to the largely male U.S. Court of Appeals for the District of Columbia Circuit, and in 1993, she became the second woman to sit on the Supreme Court, the highest court in the land and the final word on cases where lower courts have disagreed. Her rulings there led her to become known as a strong voice for gender equality, the rights of workers, and the separation between church and state. As both a woman and as a Jew, she never forgot what it was like to be a member of a group that faced discrimination.

To succeed throughout her life, RBG had to work harder than most of the men around her. She had to fight against the widespread assumption that women were not as capable as men. By nature shy, she had to push herself to speak up when she felt intimidated. She also had to learn not to give up when male colleagues belittled or ignored what she said.

This even happened on the Supreme Court, especially after the first female Supreme Court justice, Sandra Day O'Connor, retired and RBG was the only woman on the Court: during private deliberations male justices dismissed arguments when she brought them up only to give the same points serious consideration when one of them did. That, she said, began to improve as more women were appointed to the Court, changing the tone of discussions.

RBG was a tireless, hardworking lawyer and justice, but she also led a full and admirable personal life. She had a great marriage and partnership with her husband, Martin "Marty" Ginsburg, who died in 2010. An esteemed lawyer himself, he was proud of his wife's accomplishments and campaigned hard for her appointment to the Supreme Court. Since RBG wasn't interested in cooking (and was a terrible cook by her own admission), he was the family chef. RBG was also a caring mother to her two children and an attentive grandmother and aunt. She was a voracious reader and took great pleasure in music, particularly opera. She enjoyed fashion, dressed with artistic flair, and admired art. A visit to her chambers was like visiting a museum of art and history with a Supreme Court justice as curator and guide. Resolute yet gracious, she always sent handwritten or hand-signed thank-you notes.

In her later years RBG experienced a string of serious health issues. Yet she did not let illness define her. She worked out and lifted weights with her personal trainer to strengthen her body. She continually took on new challenges that expanded her mind, including performing on stage in nonsinging roles in opera productions.

During her later years on the Supreme Court, RBG became a role model to a nation and a world desperately in need of role models. Not only was her work praised, but this diminutively built American powerhouse became an icon of popular culture. In 2013, a young law student dubbed her "the Notorious RBG" and the nickname stuck. Books and movies about her appeared, and RBG action figures and dolls became wildly popular. Her image was (and still is) emblazoned on T-shirts, coffee mugs, pins, socks, scarves, dresses, and many other products. When asked how it felt to be a role model to a nation, she smiled mischievously and said: "On the one hand, it feels very good. On the other hand, I think I better watch myself, so that I don't do anything that would tarnish my image!"

By the time she died, RBG had joined the ranks of a small group of Americans whose deeds will not be forgotten. A national hero along the lines of Abraham Lincoln and Martin Luther King, Jr., she will, like them, be forever celebrated as a person who changed the course of American history for the better—and will be a role model for future generations.

BIBLICAL TIMES

AS A CHILD RBG LOVED ATTENDING PASSOVER SEDERS AT HER GRANDPARENTS' HOME. As Jews have for thousands of years, her family read from the Haggadah to remember how the children of Israel suffered as slaves in Egypt. They read about the heroic acts of Moses and his brother Aaron, who led the Israelites from slavery to freedom. But traditional Haggadahs didn't mention the many women who organized, prepared, and performed courageous acts to pave the way to freedom. Among these women were five great leaders: Miriam, Moses's sister, and four other women who are even less well known: Yocheved, Moses's mother; Batya, Pharaoh's daughter; and the midwives Shifra and Puah, who refused to kill Hebrew babies. RBG was passionate about including all five of these women in this book.

As an adult, RBG was hungry to learn more about heroic women in Judaism, to read biographies and letters, prayers and theology written by Jewish women throughout history. She even participated in the creation of midrash—the tradition of Jewish storytelling that illuminates aspects of the Torah, originally practiced by rabbis but now also by others.

In 2015, she proudly wrote midrash about the women of the Haggadah with her friend Rabbi Lauren Holtzblatt, the rabbi of Adas Israel Congregation in Washington, DC, the synagogue where she attended services in her later years. They wrote about how the actions of these five great leaders were models of how women can stand up together to fight inhumane actions caused by hate and ignorance.

No one knows for sure whether the Jewish exodus from Egypt actually occurred or if the women—and men—described in the Bible were real people. (They would have lived thousands of years ago and no other evidence remains, archaeological or otherwise.) Nevertheless, the story of Exodus looms large in the story of the Jewish people and all of Western civilization—and RBG wanted these women's stories—and lessons drawn from their deeds—to be known by all.

The women of the Haggadah were not the only biblical figures who captured RBG's youthful imagination. Another is Deborah, one of the most important judges in ancient Jewish history. Her story is told in detail in the Book of Judges and in other Jewish sources, although some feminist scholars suspect that more information about her, and Miriam, as well, was later lost or removed. Deborah, of course, was a source of inspiration for RBG's lifelong pursuit of justice.

MIRIAM

*Courageous Sister Who Saved
Her Brother and Her People*

ERA: The Book of Exodus (possibly thirteenth century BCE)
BIRTHPLACE: Egypt
BIRTHDATE: Unknown

***MIRIAM IS ONE OF THE MOST FAMOUS WOMEN IN THE
BIBLE AND CERTAINLY ONE OF THE GUTSIEST.*** Yet despite
the all-important role she plays in saving Moses and helping him lead their people to freedom, Miriam makes her
first appearance in the Book of Exodus without a name.
The firstborn child of Yocheved and Amram and the
older sibling of Aaron and Moses, she is simply the "sister" who watches over Moses as he floats down the Nile
River in a basket. She stands in the reeds at a distance,
watching and praying for the baby's safety.

But Miriam does far more than just observe and call
on God for help. She sets aside fears for her own safety

and reveals herself to Pharaoh's daughter, who has rescued Moses. She takes the initiative to speak up, and, thinking quickly, recommends Yocheved as a nurse for the baby, without mentioning that she is his sister and that Yocheved is his mother. Still a child herself, she shows great instincts, wisdom, and courage.

Many years pass before Miriam again appears in the Book of Exodus. By then, she is a grown woman, and Moses, at God's command, has just lifted his rod and stretched out his arm to part the waters of the Red Sea so that the Israelites can escape Pharaoh's army. After the sea swallows Pharaoh and his horsemen, Miriam pulls out a timbrel, an instrument akin to a tambourine, and leads the Israelite women in dancing. In doing so, she inspires the women to have their own special moment in history. Some modern rabbis herald this as an independent act of leadership in which Miriam doesn't simply echo Moses's words.

This time the Book of Exodus refers to her as "Miriam the prophet, Aaron's sister." She is considered a prophet because the Torah says that as a child she foresaw that Yocheved was "destined to bear a son who will save Israel." According to one midrash—a story told by early rabbis to illuminate aspects of the Torah—the house filled with light when Moses was born, and Amram rose and kissed Miriam on the head, saying, "My daughter, your prophecy has been fulfilled." But when the new pharaoh decreed that male babies born to the Hebrew slaves should be killed, Amram doubted Miriam's vision. Through her brave intervention with Pharaoh's daughter, the midrash continues, Miriam made it possible for her full prophecy to come true.

Miriam's story doesn't end when the waters of the Red Sea part. She helps the struggling tribes in the desert find water, and the well at the encampment at Kadesh is known as Miriam's Well. When she dies, it dries up and the Israelites are left without water.

TODAY: To provide women with a place at the Passover seder, many families now place a kos Miryam, Miriam's cup, on the table beside the cup of Elijah. The cup is filled with water to symbolize her connection to water and her miraculous well.

YOCHEVED

*Defiant Mother Who Saved
Her Son and Her People*

ERA: The Book of Exodus (possibly thirteenth century BCE)
BIRTHPLACE: Egypt
BIRTHDATE: Unknown

*YOCHEVED WAS THE MOTHER OF MOSES, WHO LED THE
ISRAELITES OUT OF EGYPT AND IS ONE OF THE MOST
PIVOTAL FIGURES IN ALL OF JEWISH HISTORY.* He might
never have lived past infancy if it were not for her bravery. She was determined to save him and defy Pharaoh's
decree that male babies born to Hebrew slaves be killed.
That was easier said than done, but she was a very
resourceful woman.

First, she hid the baby for three months. Then, when
he was too big to hide any longer, she fashioned a basket
out of bulrushes, waterproofed it, and placed it among
the reeds in the Nile River, where it was protected. She

sent her daughter, Miriam, one of Moses's two older siblings, to watch as the basket floated downstream to the spot where Pharaoh's daughter Batya was bathing.

The baby was rescued by Batya, who spoke with Miriam and agreed to hire a Hebrew wet nurse to take care of the baby. The biblical account says that Miriam brought Yocheved to Batya, and as a result, Yocheved was able to nurse her own child. Later, she returned him to Batya, who adopted him, named him Moses, and raised him as a member of the Egyptian royal family.

How long did Yocheved get to keep her child? We don't know. The biblical story says she raised the baby until he had "grown," though in those days that could have meant after he was old enough to be weaned—about two years old—or much longer. What the story also doesn't say, but what can be guessed, is that at some point Yocheved must have told him of his true identity, allowing him to sympathize with the plight of the suffering Israelite slaves. In doing so, she helped him discover his life's mission. When as an adult Moses summoned the courage and determination to lead the Israelites out of Egypt to freedom, he was following his mother's example of fighting for the life and survival of the Jewish people.

Yocheved's deeds extended beyond her own family. She was a nurse for the Israelite community in Egypt.

She took pride in caring for newborns and their mothers at tremendous personal risk. She and Miriam also collected baby clothes and food and distributed them to the poor. Her compassion and wisdom are respected and praised in Jewish texts.

Yocheved lived a long time, even longer than Moses. Unlike her children Miriam, Aaron, and Moses—all of them considered prophets—she entered the land of Canaan. According to Jewish legend, she is buried in the Tomb of the Matriarchs, in Tiberias, Israel.

TODAY: Many people add an orange to the seder plate as a symbol to remember the heroic women of Jewish history and all marginalized people who, like Yocheved, have been left out of the traditional retelling of the Passover story.

BATYA

Daughter of Pharaoh Who Rescued a Hebrew Baby and Devoted Convert

ERA: *The Book of Exodus (possibly thirteenth century BCE)*
BIRTHPLACE: *Egypt*
BIRTHDATE: *Unknown*

IN THE BOOK OF EXODUS, SHE IS SIMPLY KNOWN AS BAT-PHARAOH, "DAUGHTER OF PHARAOH," BUT LATER JEWISH TEXTS CALL HER BATYA, LITERALLY MEANING "DAUGHTER OF GOD." She was the daughter of the new Egyptian pharaoh, the one who decreed that all male babies born to the Hebrew slaves should be killed, and she is one of the women central to Moses's survival. For it is she who, while bathing in the Nile River, noticed a floating basket, asked her maid to fetch it, and discovered a crying Israelite baby, whose mother, Yocheved, had taken this desperate measure to save her son's life. Batya knew it was a Hebrew baby, and according to the Book of

Exodus, she made a decision that changed history: She defied her father's decree and rescued him.

Some rabbis say that Batya ignored her maids when they told her that it wasn't her place to rescue Moses. There's a midrash—a story told by the early rabbis—that says angels came down from the heavens, sent by God to oppose the maids who tried to stop Batya. This was interpreted as a divine sign that Batya was a righteous ally of the Jewish people.

She is considered righteous not only for defying her father and saving Moses but because after speaking to Miriam, who had been hiding nearby in the reeds to see what would become of her baby brother, Batya agreed to hire a Hebrew woman, Yocheved, as a wet nurse for the baby. Later, when Moses was weaned, Batya adopted him and loved him as her own son. It was Batya who named him Moses (Moshe), saying, "I drew him out (meshitihu) of the water." The Hebrew word māšāh means "to draw."

Batya is one of a small group of biblical women who have become known as the "devout converts." The Bible tells how Batya, not wanting to be associated with her father's cruel ways, stopped worshipping Egyptian idols. The Book of Chronicles says she left her life of wealth and ease to marry Mered, a member of the tribe of Judah, had children with him, and refers to her as a Jewess. Along with the other Jews, she follows Moses out of Egypt.

Batya was able to empathize with people different from herself and was willing to take risks in order to do what she believed was right. Without her decision to save a Hebrew infant, the Israelites might have remained slaves in Egypt.

TODAY: Although Batya is a popular Hebrew name in Israel, the story of this empathetic and brave Egyptian woman who saved Moses is still absent from most seder discussions.

SHIFRA AND PUAH

Midwives Who Outwitted the Egyptian Ruler

ERA: *The Book of Exodus (possibly thirteenth century BCE)*
BIRTHPLACE: *Egypt*
BIRTHDATE: *Unknown*

THE NAMES OF THE MIDWIVES SHIFRA AND PUAH COME UP ONLY ONCE IN THE BOOK OF EXODUS. Yet if not for the bravery of these two women, the Jewish people might not exist.

In the Book of Exodus, Pharaoh commanded Shifra and Puah to kill all male children born to the Israelites in Egypt. They courageously refused to do his bidding. Instead, they told Pharaoh that Hebrew women were so vigorous in their ability to give birth that by the time the midwives could intervene, the babies were already born and hidden. The story goes on to say that God was pleased with their actions and made them prosper.

Rabbis explain that this biblical moment is important because in outwitting the Egyptian ruler, Shifra and Puah stood up for what was right according to God and defied the authority of an evil leader. As a result of their bravery, Moses survived and was ultimately able to lead the Israelites out of slavery in Egypt to receive the Ten Commandments on Mount Sinai.

Who were Shifra and Puah, and were these their real names? No one knows for sure. But that hasn't stopped rabbis from debating their identity for millennia. Some believe that they were a mother-daughter duo—perhaps Yocheved and Miriam. Others maintain that they were a daughter-in-law and mother-in-law team, perhaps Yocheved and her older son Aaron's wife, Elisheva. Still other scholars insist that Shifra and Puah weren't Israelites at all but rather Egyptian midwives who assisted Hebrew women in childbirth. Whoever they were, what they did is more important: They risked their lives to save the lives of newborns and helped ensure the survival of the Jewish people.

TODAY: The dedication and heroism of these midwives, who were willing to stand up to Pharaoh, are still underappreciated and should be the topic of far more Seder conversations.

DEBORAH

*Respected Judge, Leader,
Warrior, and Prophet*

ERA: 1107 BCE–1067 BCE
BIRTHPLACE: Ancient Israel
BIRTHDATE: 1107 BCE, according to the Bible

DEBORAH LIVED IN A TROUBLED TIME. Oppressed by their neighbors, the Canaanites lived in wretched conditions and in a constant state of fear. Gone were the proud days of the prophet Joshua, who a century or so earlier had led the Israelite tribes and conquered the land of Israel.

During this period the tribes chose a judge to lead them. The judge was selected by merit and not on the basis of heredity. According to the Book of Judges, Deborah was the fourth judge after the death of Joshua. The Book of Judges doesn't mention where she was born, but based on geographic evidence, historians believe that she was an Ephraimite—a member of the Hebrew tribe of Ephraim in the northern part of Israel. All the Bible says about her personal life is that she was married to a man named Lapidoth.

As a judge, Deborah considered what people had to say before deciding on the best course of action for them. Sometimes this involved making judgments to settle people's disputes. She held court under a date palm tree called the "palm of Deborah," between the towns of Ramah and Bethel. One of only seven female prophets named in the Bible, she was praised for being guided in her judgments by God.

But Deborah was more than a judge. She led an extraordinary life as a leader and warrior. Passionate about freedom for the Israelites, Deborah planned a revolt and ordered an influential Israelite, Barak, to lead ten thousand soldiers up Mount Tabor to fight the Canaanite king's much larger army. Barak gathered the men but refused to go to war without Deborah, believing that only with her inspiration and the help of God could the Israelites win against such great odds. Deborah agreed, prophesying that the glory of the victory would belong to a woman. The war is called Deborah's War.

Afterward, she is said to have written the "Song of Deborah," a poem in the Book of Judges that recounts the victory at Mount Tabor. The poem mentions Jael, another woman, who single-handedly killed the Canaan-ite army general. The defeat of the Canaanites, made possible by the actions of two women, led to forty years of peace.

Deborah is the most powerful woman to appear in the Hebrew Bible and the one most respected by men for her talents and achievements. Her greatness has inspired Jewish women—and men—for millennia and continues to do so.

TODAY: *Deborah remains one of the strongest and clearest biblical role models for both girls and boys. But while there are now more female judges, political leaders, and military generals, all these professions remain dominated by men.*

ANCIENT ISRAEL

Ancient historians rarely recorded the accomplishments of women, and when they did, strong women were often portrayed as villains or flawed characters. Queen Salome Alexandra, however, was an exception. She is praised by rabbis in the Talmud—the book that codified Jewish oral law—and by the Roman historian Flavius Josephus, and for good reason. Queen Salome Alexandra was one of the last of the long series of monarchs who ruled over the various kingdoms of ancient Israel for nearly one thousand years. As you will see, she plays a critical role in Jewish history.

SALOME ALEXANDRA

Queen of the Jews and Wise Leader

139 BCE–67 BCE

ERA: Ancient Israel
BIRTHPLACE: The Kingdom of Judea
BIRTHDATE: 139 BCE

FEW PEOPLE TODAY KNOW THAT ANCIENT ISRAEL HAD A POWERFUL QUEEN WHO RULED JUDEA FOR NINE CRITICAL YEARS OF JEWISH HISTORY. Her Hebrew name was Shlomtzion, meaning "peace of Zion" or "wholeness of Zion," but she is better known by her Greek name, Salome Alexandra. She was a member of the Hasmonean dynasty, which descended from the family of Judas Maccabee, whose defeat of the Seleucid Empire in 164 BCE inspired the story of Hanukkah.

Salome Alexandra ascended to the throne after the death of her husband, King Alexander Yannae, in 76 BCE. Although it was rare for a woman to inherit the reins of power, the king, on his deathbed, chose her to succeed him instead of either of the couple's two sons.

During her lifetime, the Second Temple still stood in Jerusalem, but Roman influence in the region was growing. The Judeans themselves were divided between two rival Jewish sects—the Sadducees, who favored keeping power in the hands of Temple priests, and the Pharisees, a smaller group of independent thinkers who argued that God could and should be worshipped even away from the Temple and outside Jerusalem.

While he was alive, her husband favored the Sadducees and persecuted the Pharisees. Salome Alexandra, however, was sympathetic to the Pharisees and when she became queen, she reversed her husband's policy. She led campaigns for increased literacy and judicial reform, and reorganized the Sanhedrin, the highest Jewish court. In the process, she removed Sadducee sages from important positions in the government and the court, replacing them with Pharisees.

This turned out to be a smart move. Pharisee ideas laid the foundations for the emergence of rabbinical Judaism many centuries later. Rabbinical Judaism allowed rabbis to interpret the laws of the Torah to provide guidance to the Jewish people after the Second Temple was destroyed in 70 CE and is credited with helping Judaism survive centuries of exile.

As queen, Salome Alexandra is also famous for bringing a brief golden age of peace and stability to the Kingdom of Judea. She was a skilled leader and one of the most effective mediators and politicians of the time. She is credited with bringing prosperity to the realm; it was written that during her reign, "the fertility of the soil was so great that the grains of wheat grew as large as kidney beans; oats as large as olives; and lentils as large as gold denarii."

Salome Alexandra was the last monarch to die while the Kingdom of Judea remained independent. After her death in 67 BCE, her sons battled each other for power, and in 37 BCE the dynasty came to an end when Judea fell to the Romans.

TODAY: While Shlomtzion's reign remains well regarded today, relatively few women have served in the highest positions of the Israeli government since the founding of the modern State of Israel in 1948. Only one, Golda Meir, served as prime minister.

SIXTEENTH CENTURY

AS THE CENTURIES ROLLED ON, WOMEN'S VOICES CONTINUED TO BE CONSPICUOUSLY ABSENT FROM RECORDED HISTORY. But there were, again, exceptions. One was Gracia Mendes Nasi, who reached a level of visibility unusual for a woman—particularly a Jewish woman during the Inquisition. The Inquisition was a centuries-long attempt by the Catholic Church to root out beliefs that it considered heresy. This ugly and painful chapter in human affairs had a cataclysmic impact at the time and still has ripple effects today. It began on the Iberian Peninsula and no people were more affected by it than the Sephardi Jews who lived in Portugal and Spain at the end of the sixteenth century. In Lisbon, where Gracia was born, and throughout the Christian world, Jews were persecuted, driven out of their homes and countries, and murdered en masse. Although little is known of her childhood, the later years of Gracia's life were well documented.

GRACIA MENDES NASI

Visionary Shipping Magnate Who
Helped Jews Find Safe Places to Live

1510–1569

BIRTHPLACE: *Lisbon, Portugal*
BIRTHDATE: *1510*

GRACIA CAME INTO THE WORLD WITH TWO NAMES: HER JEWISH ONE— THE SPANISH EQUIVALENT OF HANNAH— AND HER CHRISTIAN ONE, BEATRICE. That is because Gracia was born eighteen years after the disastrous year of 1492, when Spain expelled all of its Jews and her family fled to neighboring Portugal. But their hope of continuing to live as Jews was dashed when they, and the rest of the country's Jews, were forced to convert to Catholicism. So in public, Gracia, her parents, and her sister went to church and celebrated Christian holidays. At home, they secretly practiced Judaism and longed for a land where they could live openly as Jews. Jews such as Gracia were known as *conversos* (Spanish for "converts").

Gracia was smart and well-read, and at age eighteen, she married a wealthy trader from another prominent Lisbon *converso* family. He died ten years later, leaving her with an infant daughter and his half of his family's international shipping business. Around the same time, life became even harder for Portugal's *conversos*— with the onset of the Inquisition, they were persecuted despite their conversion to Catholicism. Gracia fled north to Antwerp (now in Belgium) where she used her company's business contacts to secretly set up and fund an escape network that helped Jews leave Portugal and Spain.

Already one of the world's wealthiest women, Gracia became even richer when her husband's brother and business partner died. He not only left his half of the business to her, he also named her principal executor of the family estate, an extremely rare appointment for women of the era. She was a shrewd businesswoman, and with persecution of *conversos* on the rise in Antwerp as well, she wisely transferred the family's assets to Italy, where for the first time in her life, she was able to live openly as a Jew. There she set to work creating and supporting institutions to aid Jews who had managed to flee the Inquisition. Beloved because of her philanthropy, people began to call her Doña (Lady in Spanish) Gracia.

Anti-Semitism was spreading, and in time, the Italian city-states, too, grew hostile to Jews. This time Gracia moved her assets to Constantinople, the capital of the Ottoman Empire. From there, she conducted business and again used her fortune to establish synagogues, yeshivas, libraries, and charities for her fellow Jewish refugees. Ever in search of safe havens for Jews, she also turned her attention to Palestine, then under Ottoman control. Centuries before Austro-Hungarian writer and political activist Theodor Herzl famously began to promote the establishment of a Jewish state, Gracia negotiated a deal with Sultan Suleiman granting her family the ruins of the city of Tiberias, in what is now northern Israel, to develop into a new center of Jewish life, trade, and learning. She donated large sums of money to rebuild Tiberias into a thriving Jewish settlement. Sadly, after both she and the sultan died, the settlement fell into decline and failed. Still, stories of Gracia's vision and great generosity lived on.

TODAY: *After centuries of relative obscurity, Gracia is once again renowned, and in 2010, Israel issued a state medal and stamp honoring the 500th anniversary of her birth.*

SEVENTEENTH CENTURY

IN THE LATE 1580S, SOME SEPHARDI JEWS FLEEING THE INQUISITION ARRIVED IN HAMBURG, A CITY-STATE IN WHAT IS TODAY NORTHERN GERMANY. Ashkenazi Jews, also in search of a safe place to live, settled there soon after. But wherever they were from, life wasn't easy for Jews in the German states. There was no formal Inquisition, but the seventeenth century was marked by religious wars between the followers of Martin Luther, a monk who had tried to fight corruption in the Catholic Church and instead ended up launching the Protestant Reformation, and followers of the pope in Rome. As was often the case, one of the few things both sides could agree on was their dislike of the Jews, and many anti-Jewish edicts and actions were issued.

Meanwhile, women, whether Catholic, Protestant, or Jewish, had few freedoms; their only choice in life was to run the household, bear and raise children, and, if they were affluent, manage the servants. Few attended school, and when they did, what they could study was limited. One entrepreneurial businesswoman of this period, Glückel of Hameln, stands out. Not because historians wrote about her—they didn't—but because she put pen to paper and wrote her life story in her own words.

GLÜCKEL OF HAMELN

Savvy Businesswoman Who Wrote Her Own Story

1646–1724

BIRTHPLACE: The independent city-state of Hamburg, now part of Germany
BIRTHDATE: 1646

HER NAME IS DERIVED FROM GLÜCK, *THE GERMAN TRANSLATION OF THE HEBREW NAME "MAZAL," MEANING "GOOD FORTUNE," AND GLÜCKEL WAS INDEED FORTU-NATE TO GROW UP IN A WEALTHY FAMILY IN HAMBURG.* Her father was a diamond trader and her mother also worked in the family business, which was highly unusual at that time. Glückel was also lucky in that her parents believed that girls as well as boys should be educated. Although girls weren't permitted to study the Torah, she attended a Jewish school and learned Hebrew.

Nevertheless, her parents had very traditional ideas

when it came to their daughters' lives. When Glückel was twelve, they arranged for her marriage. Two years later she was married, and by fifteen she was pregnant with the first of fourteen children, twelve of whom would survive to adulthood. Like other Jewish housewives of the time, Glückel raised the children and managed the household.

But she was also a savvy businesswoman. Her husband, like her parents, traded in jewelry and precious stones and made loans and managed financial transactions. Not only did he seek Glückel's advice, but she kept the books, interviewed new business partners, and drafted agreements. Her role and influence went far beyond what was allowed most women. When her husband died she was forty-four, and he left all of his assets to her, an extraordinary action for the time. "My wife, she knows everything," he said on his deathbed. "Let her do as she has done until now."

As a widow, Glückel continued to care for her children and run the household but took over all responsibility for the business, traveling throughout Europe to attend trade fairs and even opening a factory. Under her control, the business flourished and she accumulated a substantial fortune, making it possible for her to arrange good marriages for her children.

Two years after her husband's death, Glückel took

to writing about her life as an outlet for her grief. That memoir, written in Yiddish and growing to seven volumes, was meant only for her children, but her descendants published it in 1896, almost 150 years after her death. It's a good thing they did: autobiographical writing was uncommon during her lifetime, and her words are a rare window into the daily lives of affluent Jews in the seventeenth and early eighteenth centuries. That Glückel was a woman—and a Jew—makes the book even more extraordinary.

Glückel fended off many suitors, but once her children were grown, she remarried, which meant that her new husband controlled her property. He wasn't an astute businessman, and when he died, he left her penniless. Nonetheless, Glückel's account of her life is filled with assertions of her strong faith and her gratitude for her many blessings, and her accomplishments are remembered to this day.

TODAY: In recent years, there has been renewed appreciation of Glückel's importance, and a number of new English translations of her memoirs have been published.

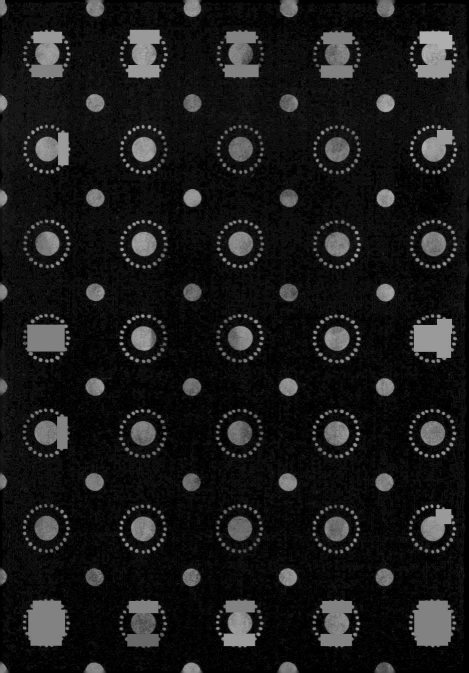

EIGHTEENTH CENTURY

WE NOW TURN TO A WOMAN BORN ON A FARAWAY CONTINENT IN A BRAND-NEW COUNTRY, THE UNITED STATES OF AMERICA— REBECCA GRATZ. We know more about her than about many of the women who came before her because by the eighteenth century newspapers and periodicals, both religious and secular, had ushered in a new age of information in Europe and America. Most articles, of course, were written by and about men, but the speeches and deeds of preeminent women were also documented. In addition, Rebecca recorded her thoughts and observations in prolific correspondence, much of which survived her. On top of all of this, she was the inspiration for a character in one of the great novels of her time, written by the British writer Sir Walter Scott. RBG believed that no book about Jewish women would be complete without Rebecca.

REBECCA GRATZ

Founder and Organizer of America's
First Social Services Organizations

1781–1869

BIRTHPLACE: *Lancaster, Pennsylvania*
BIRTHDATE: *March 4, 1781*

REBECCA GRATZ GREW UP IN PHILADELPHIA AT AN EXCITING TIME IN AMERICAN HISTORY. Five years after the signing of the Declaration of Independence, the new nation was emerging from the Revolutionary War. Philadelphia, Greek for "city of brotherly love," was the nation's first capital and was known as a city where Americans of different religions could mingle and worship freely without restrictions.

Born into a wealthy and respected Jewish family, Rebecca, along with her parents and siblings, participated fully in the city's vibrant political and social life. She was the seventh of ten children, five of them girls.

Her parents believed that their daughters should be as well educated as their sons and made sure Rebecca and her sisters had every opportunity. An avid reader and a talented writer, Rebecca chose to dedicate herself to community service. When she was twenty, she and her mother and sisters launched a nondenominational organization to aid poor women and children. Known as the Female Association of Philadelphia for the Relief of Women and Children in Reduced Circumstances, it was unique in bringing together women from different faiths and for being an entirely women-run organization.

As the organization's secretary, Rebecca insisted that the treasurer be unmarried. This was not an arbitrary rule since at the time men controlled their wives' assets. This meant married women could not hold property in their own names, and they could not enter into contracts or bring lawsuits. Requiring the treasurer to be unmarried safeguarded the group's funds and ensured that no husband could assert a right to manage or divert its money.

Rebecca cared deeply about Judaism and Philadelphia's Jewish community. In 1819, she founded the Female Hebrew Benevolent Society to provide social services to Jewish women and children—and she led it for forty years. In 1838, she started the Hebrew Sunday School Society of Philadelphia and was school superintendent for almost twenty years. The coeducational Philadelphia school became the model for Jewish religious schools across the country. She also helped establish the nation's first Jewish orphanage and aided Jewish women in other cities in launching similar schools and orphanages. Organizations modeled on those Rebecca founded continue to serve communities throughout the United States today.

Rebecca never married, although she raised six nephews and nieces after one of her sisters died. Beloved in Philadelphia, she became a role model for Jewish American women everywhere. Through her achievements, she showed that women could both maintain their Jewish identity and fit into American society. She was so well known that she was the inspiration for the character Rebecca in Sir Walter Scott's classic novel *Ivanhoe.* Scott's Rebecca is the first favorable depiction of a Jew in English fiction. He portrays her as a sympathetic young Jewish woman who is beautiful, courageous, virtuous, and noble of character, just like the real one.

TODAY: Rebecca remains one of the best known Jewish figures in American history, and a book, Letters of Rebecca Gratz, published in 1929, provides an unusually extensive look into her life and the country at the time.

NINETEENTH CENTURY

RBG WAS QUITE KNOWLEDGEABLE ABOUT MANY OF THE EXTRAORDINARY WOMEN BORN IN THE NINETEENTH CENTURY. A few of them were actively shaking up the world during her lifetime and left deep impressions on her. Others loomed large in her childhood, which was not all that long after American women won the right to vote. Two she referred to as early role models—Emma Lazarus, author of the poem engraved on the Statue of Liberty's base, and Henrietta Szold, the passionate Zionist who founded Hadassah, the well-known organization of Jewish women.

She expressed strong opinions about some of them. For example, she was proud that Golda Meir was Israel's prime minister but disappointed that no other women had yet followed in her footsteps to lead the Jewish state. RBG, who would have loved to be an opera star had she had the talent, also thought it tragic that the pianist and composer Fanny Mendelssohn was not permitted to perform in public or publish the music she composed. RBG also had a special place in her heart for Gertrude Berg, one of the most popular radio and television stars of the first half of the twentieth century. She had fond childhood memories of listening to Gertrude's radio show, in which the writer, producer, and comedic actor starred as the fictional Molly Goldberg, the matriarch of a Jewish immigrant family. Long before she heard the word *feminism,* she admired Gertrude's assertiveness at a time when assertiveness was not considered a positive feminine quality. She also observed that Gertrude was a proud working-woman, despite the prevailing view that a woman shouldn't work outside the home because people might think her husband wasn't able to support his family. Even as a girl, RBG thought this was silly.

ERNESTINE ROSE

*Trailblazing Feminist and Fighter
for the Abolition of Slavery*

1810–1892

BIRTHPLACE: *Piotrkow, Poland*
BIRTHDATE: *January 13, 1810*

*ERNESTINE ROSE WAS THE ONLY CHILD OF A PROMINENT
BUT STRICT POLISH RABBI, AND BY AGE FIVE, SHE WAS
PUMMELING HIM WITH THEOLOGICAL QUESTIONS, SUCH
AS "WHY DOES GOD LET PEOPLE SUFFER?"* Although
she clearly had a sharp and inquiring mind, her father
ignored her questions and refused to send her to school.
He did, however, permit her to study Torah and Talmud,
and hired a tutor to teach her Hebrew. At age fourteen,
Ernestine asked him why women were assumed to be
inferior to men in Judaism, and with no good answer
forthcoming, she rebelled against the Jewish texts and
traditions that supported this belief. This question

became all the more urgent when she was sixteen and her mother died, leaving her a small fortune. Without even asking her, her father promised her inheritance to a man he'd arranged for her to marry.

This was his right under Jewish custom, but Ernestine was outraged and did what was unimaginable at the time: she took her father to Polish civil court. She acted as her own attorney and convinced the judge to rule in her favor, gaining both her inheritance and her freedom. It was her freedom that mattered to her: she gave the lion's share of her inheritance to her father, keeping just enough to go to Berlin and to invent a specially treated chemical paper that, when burned, dispelled cooking odors in crowded tenements, enabling her to support herself. After traveling through Holland, Belgium, and France, she moved to London where she met and married a thoughtful silversmith who shared her values of social reform. In 1836 she and her husband settled in New York City and opened a small jewelry and perfume store.

The pursuit of justice became Ernestine's full-time passion. Even before suffragists Elizabeth Cady Stanton and Susan B. Anthony began agitating for women's rights, Ernestine was crisscrossing the country advocating religious tolerance, public education, and equality for women. Audiences loved her. An inspirational speaker

with a flair for humor, she was known as an intellectual force for women's suffrage. She was a strong believer
that women's rights and the abolition of slavery should
be approached as one issue, a controversial proposition
at the time. "Emancipation from every kind of human
bondage is my principle," she said.

Ernestine also lobbied for married women to be able
to own and buy property in their own names—and to
have the same guardianship rights of children that men
had in case of divorce. At the time, women could with
difficulty leave a bad marriage, but the price was giving up their children. Thanks in part to her efforts, New
York State gave these rights to married women in 1849.
Twenty years later, she joined Stanton and Anthony in
founding the National Woman Suffrage Association.
While she—and the other founders—would not live to
see the 1920 passage of the Nineteenth Amendment to
the U.S. Constitution giving women the right to vote,
they played a crucial role in laying the groundwork.

Susan B. Anthony recognized Ernestine as one
of the foremothers of the nineteenth-century wom-
en's rights movement in America, but despite her early
and prominent role, Ernestine is not as well-known as
other suffragist leaders. Some believe that is because
she retired to England in 1869; others attribute it to the

fact that she was an immigrant and a Jew. While Ernestine did not believe in God, she was a fierce defender of the Jewish people and spoke out against anti-Semitic and anti-immigrant attitudes that were then prevalent throughout the United States. Despite the lack of recognition, her lifelong insistence on advocating for justice helped change the destiny of millions of women of all faiths and backgrounds.

TODAY: In recent decades, feminist historians have been rediscovering Ernestine's critical early role, and in 1998 the Ernestine Rose Society was founded to revive her legacy. The marker at her gravesite in London was restored in 2002.

FANNY MENDELSSOHN

*Talented Pianist and Composer
Overshadowed by the
Success of Her Famous Brother*

1805–1847

BIRTHPLACE: Hamburg, Germany
BIRTHDATE: November 14, 1805

FANNY MENDELSSOHN'S GREAT GIFT FOR MUSIC WAS OBVIOUS TO EVERYONE IN HER FAMILY. When she was thirteen, as a surprise for her father, she performed twenty-four Bach preludes on the piano from memory. She loved to compose, too, writing her first known song for her father on his birthday.

But it was her brother Felix, three years younger, who rose to fame at age nine after making his public debut in their hometown of Berlin, Germany. Fanny was happy for her brother; the two had taken piano lessons together since they were small and were inseparable. She was also envious. Although some of their teachers considered her the more talented pianist, the children's father refused to permit Fanny to play in public or to publish her music. He recognized her talent and encouraged her love of music but expected his daughter to grow up to devote her full attention to her husband and children, as did most women in the 1880s. Music, he told her, could be only an "ornament" for a woman.

Felix adored his sister but agreed with his father. Since she was very close to both of them, she respected their wishes. Fanny married an open-minded painter who encouraged her musical endeavors, and they had a son, whom she named Sebastian Ludwig Felix after her favorite composers, Johann Sebastian Bach, Ludwig van Beethoven, and her brother. In the privacy of her home, Fanny continued composing, writing nearly five hundred works, including the well-known *Easter* Sonata. She was also a prolific songwriter and orchestrated chamber music, cantatas, and a variety of works for piano and voice.

Since she did not publish her music under her own name, Felix published some of her compositions under his. This led to an embarrassing moment during a performance for England's Queen Victoria. One of Fanny's songs, the queen declared, was her favorite

"Felix Mendelssohn" song, and Felix had to confess that his sister had written the song.

Only after their parents died did Felix agree that Fanny could publish under her own name. But she never had the chance to become as famous as her brother. She died of a stroke at age forty-one. Felix, devastated by her death, died six months later and was buried by her side. Only with time has her work begun to be recognized and given the respect it deserves.

TODAY: In 2010, the <u>Easter</u> Sonata, a major piano work attributed to Felix, was determined to have been written by Fanny. It was performed under her name for the first time in 2012.

EMMA LAZARUS

*Poet Moved by the Plight of
Immigrants Whose Words Continue
to Inspire America*

1849–1887

BIRTHPLACE: *New York City*
BIRTHDATE: *July 22, 1849*

EMMA LAZARUS FELL IN LOVE WITH WRITING AT A YOUNG AGE. She composed her first poem when she was eleven and at fourteen wrote a collection of poems inspired by the Civil War, which was still raging. The collection was published as a book three years later.

Emma was fortunate to be born into one of the oldest and wealthiest Sephardic Portuguese Jewish families in America. Her parents not only encouraged her talent, but had the means to make sure she had the best private tutors and received a strong classical education. Growing up in upper-class circles in New York City and Newport,

Rhode Island, she was also well acquainted with many of the most important literary, artistic, and political figures of the time.

In addition to composing poetry, Emma wrote plays and a novel, and, fluent in several languages, she translated published collections of poetry by well-known French, German, and Italian writers. Her work was praised by celebrated writers such as Ralph Waldo Emerson in Massachusetts and George Eliot in England.

Emma could have devoted all of her time to literary endeavors, but in 1881 she was moved by the plight of thousands of impoverished Ashkenazi Jews, fleeing anti-Jewish persecution and poverty in Russia, who began arriving in New York City. She took up their cause not only with her pen, but by helping to establish a school to teach them job skills.

These immigrants—and the extreme prejudice they faced in New York—kindled in Emma a new interest in her Jewish heritage, and for the first time, she studied the Bible, Hebrew, Judaism, and Jewish history. She became an advocate for a Jewish homeland before the effort to establish a Jewish state in Israel became a movement. And she became a tireless opponent of anti-Semitism: In her *Songs of a Semite,* written in 1882, her most famous full-length work, Emma celebrated the resilience of the Jewish people.

But Emma is best known for the poem that she wrote to help raise funds to construct a pedestal for the Statue of Liberty. She called it "The New Colossus"—named after a statue that in ancient times welcomed newcomers to the Greek island of Rhodes. The last lines of the poem read:

Give me your tired, your poor,
Your huddled masses yearning to breathe free,
The wretched refuse of your teeming shore.
Send these the homeless, tempest-tost to me,
I lift my lamp beside the golden door!

Nearly one and a half centuries later, these words are familiar to most Americans. That is because in 1903 they were etched on a bronze plaque on the Statue of Liberty's pedestal, and they have greeted every immigrant arriving by ship in New York Harbor since then.

Sadly, Emma never saw the plaque because she died of cancer at age thirty-eight. But even today, her inspirational poem continues to define America's open-hearted embrace of immigrants.

TODAY: As immigration remains a major issue of debate in the United States, Emma's "The New Colossus" is still frequently quoted and is as relevant as ever.

LILLIAN WALD

*Champion of Community
Healthcare for the Poor*

1867–1940

BIRTHPLACE: Cincinnati, Ohio
BIRTHDATE: March 10, 1867

*THE DAUGHTER OF PROSPEROUS JEWISH IMMIGRANTS
FROM GERMANY AND POLAND, LILLIAN WALD WAS BORN
INTO A FAMILY THAT WAS ABLE TO PROVIDE HER WITH
EVERYTHING SHE NEEDED.* Her father ran a successful
optical business and her mother was warm, kind, and
loving. The homes Lillian grew up in, first in Ohio and
then in Rochester, New York, were filled with books
and music.

Lillian was also fortunate in her education. She
attended a top girls' school in Rochester, where she
excelled in almost every subject, then went to nursing
school in New York City. After working as a nurse at the

New York Juvenile Asylum, she enrolled in the Woman's Medical College, founded by Elizabeth Blackwell, the first woman to graduate from medical school in the United States.

While in medical school, Lillian volunteered to teach a course in home nursing for immigrants at a school in New York's Lower East Side. One morning, the daughter of one of her students came to ask Lillian for help. She followed the girl to her family's tenement, where she found her student lying in a bed drenched with blood. Lillian's eyes were opened to the health needs of those who could not afford to pay for doctors. "That morning's experience was a baptism of fire," wrote Lillian later. "Deserted were the laboratory and academic work of college. I never returned to them . . . I rejoiced that I had a training in the care of the sick."

Convinced that poverty was a social issue and not a personal failing, Lillian threw herself into helping the city's poor. She established the Henry Street Settlement, a neighborhood public health center that became a model for community service throughout America. Her work in the slums of New York brought her face-to-face with the link between poverty and disease, a connection that led her to establish the field of community nursing. She believed that all sick people, rich and poor, deserved access to quality healthcare, and to be taught how to protect themselves from deadly contagious diseases. Indigent children, in particular, died at too high a rate and deserved a better chance of survival.

Lillian's innovative approach to community health included placing nurses in public schools and setting up school lunch programs and special needs classes, all things we take for granted today. She also established New York's visiting nurse service, which provided house calls to the sick and was the world's first public nursing system.

As Lillian saw it, healthcare was deeply tied to the need for other social reforms. She championed women's suffrage and safer working conditions for women, and lobbied for child labor laws. Civil rights was another of her burning passions; the Henry Street Settlement made a point of welcoming and helping people of all races, which was controversial at the time. Lillian was also one of the founders of the National Association for the Advancement of Colored People (NAACP), which held its first meeting at the settlement house.

Lillian's tireless efforts and innovations transformed the way communities in America treated the poor. Once considered radical, the programs she founded are now considered essential.

TODAY: The original Henry Street Settlement in New York City that Lillian founded and ran is still open today, providing healthcare, social services, and community arts programs.

EMMY NOETHER

Mathematical Genius Who Developed the Field of Abstract Algebra

1882–1935

BIRTHPLACE: Erlangen, Germany
BIRTHDATE: March 23, 1882

EMMY NOETHER'S FAVORITE SUBJECT WAS MATH, WHICH WAS NO SURPRISE SINCE HER FATHER WAS A MATHEMATICS PROFESSOR AT THE UNIVERSITY IN THEIR HOMETOWN OF ERLANGEN, A CITY IN THE BAVARIAN REGION OF GERMANY. Although he encouraged his gifted daughter's desire to learn, a career as a mathematician was impossible for a girl. Girls weren't allowed to go to college preparatory schools or attend German universities. So Emmy went to a girls' finishing school where she excelled at languages and was certified to become a French and English teacher.

But upon graduation, she switched course and

decided to attend the university in Erlangen to study advanced mathematics. Emmy talked her way into being allowed to sit in on classes, and in 1904, she was finally accepted as a student. Three years later, she was awarded her PhD in mathematics, a stunning achievement at the time.

The next step, finding a job, turned out to be even more daunting: women were not given university positions. As a result, Emmy worked at the Mathematical Institute of Erlangen for seven years without pay or title. She assisted her father while doing her own research into computational algebra and publishing articles.

In 1915, she was invited to teach at the University of Göttingen, then the world's center for the study of mathematics. The teaching position was sabotaged by faculty members who refused to accept a woman among their ranks, so she served as assistant to David Hilbert, a renowned mathematician who recognized her brilliance and the importance of her work. She lectured under Hilbert's name, unpaid, and lived a frugal existence that bordered on poverty.

Fascinated by the mathematical conundrums of her time, she wrote a paper applying her knowledge of advanced algebra to Albert Einstein's 1915 theory of relativity. Her work solved a nagging problem, proving a revolutionary mathematical theorem (now called Noether's theorem) that changed how physicists study the universe. The paper and the lecture she gave on it caught the great physicist's attention. Albert Einstein called Emmy a "genius."

Hilbert and some of her other colleagues fought for Emmy to be made a professor, and finally, in 1919, she was permitted to lecture under her own name. Even then she was not paid. Only in 1922 was she named an "associate professor without tenure" and given a small salary. Because she was a woman—and also a Jew—she was never promoted to full professor or given tenure, which would have given her job security.

Despite the prejudices she faced, Emmy confidently led the way in developing the field of modern or "abstract" algebra. She taught and mentored many students, nicknamed "Noether's boys," and her work inspired mathematicians throughout Europe.

Although one of her brothers was also a mathematician, Emmy was the star of the family, becoming so famous she was known as "der Noether"—German for "the Noether."

Then came another blow: the Nazis came to power in 1933, forcing Emmy—and other Jews—from their jobs and making it dangerous for them to stay in Germany.

Fortunately, Emmy's work was admired worldwide, and a position was created for her in the United States at Pennsylvania's Bryn Mawr College—a school with a long tradition of preparing women for complex mathematical research.

For the first time in her life, she had female colleagues and all female students. Remembering how difficult it had been for her to become accepted as a mathematician and as a teacher, Emmy devoted herself to mentoring younger female mathematicians. She also traveled weekly to Princeton University to lecture at the Institute for Advanced Studies and to collaborate with some of America's leading mathematicians.

She died in 1935, leaving her mark on higher mathematics but never receiving the recognition she deserved. Upon her death, some of her peers called her the greatest female mathematician in history. Many mathematicians now recognize Emmy as the greatest algebraist of the twentieth century.

TODAY: The status of women in mathematics has improved since Emmy's time, but bias and discrimination remain prevalent.

ROSE SCHNEIDERMAN

*Relentless Advocate on Behalf
of Poor Working Women*

1882–1972

BIRTHPLACE: *Sawin, Poland*
BIRTHDATE: *April 6, 1882*

ROSE SCHNEIDERMAN WAS EIGHT YEARS OLD WHEN SHE AND HER FAMILY ARRIVED IN NEW YORK CITY FROM POLAND. There was little money left after the long journey, so the family moved into a tenement on the city's Lower East Side where the kitchen served as living room by day and a bedroom at night. Her father worked as a tailor and her mother took whatever jobs she found to pay the rent and put food on the table.

Three years later, Rose's father died. Left with three children and expecting another, her mother did everything she could to keep Rose, who was very bright, in school. But Rose was forced to drop out after ninth grade to help support the family. There were no laws against children working, so she became a salesgirl in a department store, then got a job in a factory sewing linings for men's caps. The shifts were long and the pay was meager, and she resented the fact that no matter how well she did her work, the best-paying positions were reserved for men.

To win better treatment for herself and her fellow workers, Rose organized a chapter of the United Cloth Hat and Cap Makers' Union. Her ability to organize and speak so impressed her coworkers—and the union's male leaders—that she became the first woman elected to be the union's delegate to the New York City Central Labor Union.

Rose threw herself into fighting for female garment workers who had no power to protect themselves, organizing union chapters and leading worker strikes. In 1911, the dire situation of seamstresses made national news after a fire at the Triangle Shirtwaist Factory in Greenwich Village in New York City killed 146 people— mostly young Italian and Jewish immigrant girls between the ages of fourteen and twenty-three. The girls had been locked in, so they couldn't escape the flames. Rose's impassioned speech at a memorial for them was so compelling that it was quoted in *The New York Times*.

"I would be a traitor to those poor burned bodies, if I were to come here to talk good fellowship. We have tried you good people of the public—and we have found you wanting," she said, adding that every week, girls working in factories were killed and maimed, and that their lives were considered cheap.

Rose became a leader of the Women's Trade Union League, a coalition of working and middle-class women, and fought for better safety standards. In addition to organizing, she campaigned for women's suffrage because, as she saw it, the power of the vote was a matter of life and death for female workers. "I think that I was born a suffragist but if I hadn't been, I'm sure that the conditions of the working girls in New York . . . would have made me one," she said. Speaking in Yiddish and English, she campaigned for suffrage and workers' rights on street corners and outside factories, standing on soap-boxes and ladders because she was only four feet, nine inches tall.

In 1920, the Nineteenth Amendment finally gave American women the right to vote, but Rose continued pushing for ways to improve the lives of women workers, even running for the U.S. Senate in 1920. Although she lost, she would go on to become influential on the national stage. In 1921, a woman she had met through her work invited her to a small, informal dinner. There she met the hostess's husband—a charming, politically ambitious young man named Franklin Delano Roosevelt. Rose and Eleanor Roosevelt became lifelong friends, and when Eleanor's husband became president of the United States in 1933, Rose became one of his advisors—and one of the few members of his brain trust who knew firsthand what working life was like. Two years later, the president named Rose as the only woman on the new National Labor Advisory Board, formed to protect the rights of workers to join together, with or without a union, to improve their wages and working conditions.

Rose later held a number of high political offices such as New York state secretary of labor, where she fought to extend the new federal retirement program called Social Security and to win equal pay for women. During the late 1930s and early 1940s, she also became deeply involved in efforts to rescue European Jews from the Nazis and to resettle them in the United States and Palestine.

Rose lived until she was ninety, writing her memoirs and traveling the country giving speeches. Whether on a soapbox, on national radio, in a large banquet hall, or in the White House, she never gave up fighting for better lives for working women and others who couldn't defend themselves.

TODAY: *Much of what Rose championed is now enshrined in American law. Nevertheless, many immigrants continue to be paid poorly and treated badly, and are forced to work in unsafe conditions.*

SARAH SCHENIRER

Self-Taught Teacher Who Created a Movement to Educate Orthodox Women

1883–1935

BIRTHPLACE: *Krakow, Poland*
BIRTHDATE: *July 15, 1883*

SARAH SCHENIRER WAS DESCENDED FROM TWO INFLU-ENTIAL HASIDIC RABBINICAL DYNASTIES, AND WAS A VERY DEVOUT CHILD. She longed to study the Torah alongside her brothers, but in Krakow, Poland, where she lived, like everywhere else at the time, girls were not taught Torah. Since women were not included in the commandment to study Torah, it was believed that there was no need for them to receive formal religious education.

Sarah's father, however, recognized her intelligence and desire to learn and provided her with religious texts translated into Yiddish, the language that the family spoke at home. He also allowed her to attend a Polish elementary school for eight years, where she learned Polish and German. Unassuming and withdrawn, she then dutifully became a seamstress, one of the few professions deemed suitable for women.

During World War I, her family moved to Vienna, where Sarah heard a sermon by a well-known rabbi about the important roles women had played throughout Jewish history. She was so inspired by this sermon that upon her return to Krakow in 1917 she founded Bais Yaakov (House of Jacob), a movement to educate Orthodox girls and young women. She believed it was important for women to have access to Jewish learning in order to understand the meaning of the holidays and to follow services, even if they were required to sit separately from men in synagogues.

In 1917, Sarah opened a kindergarten class for twenty-five girls in her sewing studio, eventually adding classes for other grades. She quickly blossomed into an inspirational teacher and charismatic leader. Within five years, seven schools with 1,040 students were affiliated with Bais Yaakov. Sarah developed curricula with material about women in Judaism to bolster the movement's legitimacy in the Orthodox community. Under her leadership, Bais Yaakov achieved broad acceptance, becoming the women's educational division of Agudat

Israel, the political arm of Orthodox Ashkenazi Jews. By 1933, when Sarah stepped down, there were 265 schools in Poland alone, educating nearly thirty-eight thousand girls.

This remarkable, mostly self-taught woman, with no formal qualifications in Jewish studies or in teaching, created a worldwide movement that forever changed the status of women's education within Orthodox Judaism. Although Sarah was married twice, she never had children. She considered her students her daughters. In return, they called their beloved teacher, "our Sarah Imeinu," which means "our mother Sarah."

TODAY: There are many opportunities for Orthodox Jewish women to study Jewish texts such as the Torah and the Talmud today. However, there are still some communities where this practice is frowned upon.

HENRIETTA SZOLD

*Scholar and Activist Who
Transformed Healthcare in Israel*

1860–1945

BIRTHPLACE: Baltimore, Maryland
BIRTHDATE: December 21, 1860

**BORN IN BALTIMORE, HENRIETTA SZOLD WAS THE ELDEST
OF EIGHT DAUGHTERS.** Her father, a rabbi and scholar,
encouraged her studies and taught her Hebrew, German,
and Jewish texts. She was a stellar student and after
high school, she became a schoolteacher, one of the few
acceptable professions for women. She worked with children during the day and started a night school to instruct
immigrants in English and job skills. Together with her
father, to whom she was close, she would go down to the
city's docks to assist new arrivals as they got off ships
from Eastern Europe and Russia.

After her father died in 1902, Henrietta moved with

her mother to New York City to attend rabbinical school. Women could not be ordained as rabbis, so before enrolling, she had to agree not to ask to be ordained as a rabbi. Her scholarship was highly respected, however, and Henrietta found other ways to work for Jewish people. A writer and translator, she was the only woman prominent in the Jewish Publication Society, which published Jewish texts and authoritative English translations of scriptures. She later became its first full-time executive secretary of publications.

Henrietta was a strong proponent for a Jewish homeland and was a Zionist before that word was coined. In 1896, one month before Theodor Herzl—the man considered "the father of Zionism"—published his first book on Zionism, Henrietta gave a speech in which she imagined a Jewish state in Palestine that could become a haven for the world's Jews. She would go on to be the only woman of her era to serve on the executive committees of America's major Zionist organizations.

In 1909, Henrietta and her mother traveled through Europe and the Middle East, then toured Palestine. While there, Henrietta observed the dismal conditions in which both Jews and Arab residents lived and was shocked by the lack of healthcare and social services. She vowed to change this and upon her return to New York, she founded Hadassah to provide healthcare to all residents of the Yishuv, or pre-Israel Palestine. Starting as a small organization of women who could give just pennies a week, it grew into the largest American Jewish women's organization.

Henrietta never hid her opinion that women should have a larger role in rabbinical Judaism. In 1916, when her mother died, she defied Jewish tradition and asserted her right to recite the mourner's Kaddish prayer. She added that she did not believe that it had ever been intended that women should not perform such duties when they could.

Henrietta moved to Palestine in 1920 to direct Hadassah's work, including the establishment of clinics and a hospital, laying the foundation for modern healthcare. She was also involved in other social and political endeavors.

In 1933, she joined Youth Aliyah, an organization that rescued up to thirty thousand children from the Nazis and brought them to Palestine. Later, when those children wrote to thank her, she answered every one of their letters.

She died at age eighty-four in Jerusalem's Hadassah Hospital, the hospital she had helped build. By then Henrietta was known as "the mother of the Yishuv."

Today in Israel, Mother's Day is celebrated on the anniversary of her death.

> **TODAY:** Hadassah, which Henrietta founded, remains one of the largest international Jewish organizations, and Hadassah Hospital is one of Jerusalem's leading medical institutions.

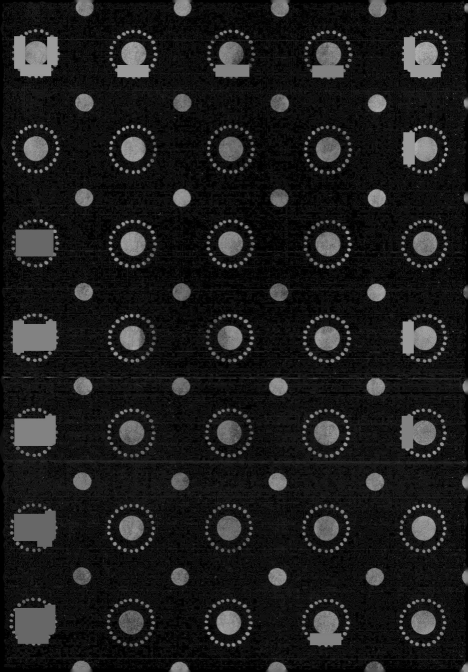

FLORENCE PRAG KAHN

*First Jewish Congresswoman
in the United States*

1866–1948

BIRTHPLACE: Salt Lake City, Utah
BIRTHDATE: November 9, 1866

FLORENCE PRAG KAHN WAS BORN IN SALT LAKE CITY, UTAH, BUT GREW UP IN THE BOOMING GOLD RUSH CITY OF SAN FRANCISCO, CALIFORNIA. Her parents, Polish immigrants, were active in the city's vibrant, growing Jewish community and civic world; Florence's father was a merchant, and her mother, a religious school and high school teacher, was one of the first Jewish and female members of the San Francisco Board of Education. Both valued a religious and secular education for their daughter, and Florence, smart, quick-witted, and driven to learn, flourished. She was one of seven women in a class of forty who graduated from the University of California, Berkeley, in 1887.

Florence wanted to pursue a law degree but her family couldn't afford the tuition, so she followed in her mother's footsteps and taught English and history for more than a decade at a San Francisco high school. In 1899 she married Julius Kahn, an actor turned lawyer and a first-term Republican member of the U.S. House of Representatives from San Francisco, with whom she had two sons. In Washington, DC, Florence assisted her husband in carrying out the duties of his office and closely followed policy debates. She also expressed her views during a two-year stint as a columnist for the *San Francisco Chronicle*. When Julius died after a long illness twelve terms later, Florence ran for his House seat and won, becoming in 1925 the first non-Christian congresswoman and the fifth woman to serve in Congress.

She proudly introduced herself as a Jew, and in her first speech before the House she observed that since Moses had conducted the world's first census, she was especially qualified to address the issue of redistribution of seats in the House based on changes in population. Admired for her wit, she was well liked by her constituents, who reelected her five times, and was respected by her male colleagues, who valued her political acumen and debate skills.

Florence was assigned to some of the House's most

powerful committees, becoming the first woman to sit on the Military Affairs Committee, and later, the first woman on the House Appropriations Committee, which helps determine how the government spends money. She successfully lobbied for economic growth in her home district, securing funds for the construction of military bases and critical infrastructure such as San Francisco's famous Golden Gate Bridge and Bay Bridge.

Although as a younger woman she had opposed women's suffrage, Florence became a powerful advocate for women in Congress. Men (and Democrats!) didn't intimidate her, and many of her colleagues backed measures she proposed to help women, including pensions for army nurses and higher wages for female government employees. Believing that women should help each other, she encouraged women to vote and to run for high political office. "There is no sex in citizenship," she once said, "and there should be none in politics."

TODAY: More women—and Jewish women—now serve in both the U.S. House of Representatives and the Senate, but overall, women are still significantly underrepresented in Congress.

GOLDA MEIR

First and Only Female
Prime Minister of Israel

1898–1978

BIRTHPLACE: *Kyiv, Ukraine*
BIRTHDATE: *May 3, 1898*

WHEN GOLDA MEIR WAS EIGHT, SHE AND HER FAMILY FLED POVERTY AND RELIGIOUS PERSECUTION IN RUSSIA AND EMIGRATED TO MILWAUKEE, WISCONSIN. A child of extraordinary energy and intelligence, she worked in her mother's grocery store, organized fundraisers to help children buy textbooks, and excelled in school. But when she graduated as valedictorian of her eighth-grade class, her parents pressured her to get married instead of attending high school. Golda refused and ran away to live with a married sister in Denver, Colorado. There she was introduced to Zionism and Morris Meyerson, a sign painter—and fell in love with both.

 123

Her parents relented, and Golda returned to Milwaukee, graduated from high school, and studied at a teachers' college. She left college, however, to pursue her true passion: the creation of a Jewish state in Palestine led by workers. In 1917, a little more than a month after Britain issued the Balfour Declaration supporting "the establishment in Palestine of a National Home for the Jewish people," Golda married Morris and in 1921, the couple sailed for Palestine.

As many new immigrants did, they settled on a kibbutz, an agricultural community built around socialist principles where everyone worked together and shared the fruits of their labor. Golda, strong and vigorous, put her organizing skills to work and thrived. Morris, however, wasn't cut out for kibbutz life, so the couple moved to Jerusalem, where Golda gave birth to two children and had a series of jobs in which she actively pursued her goal: the establishment of a state for Jews. She quickly rose up the ranks of key Jewish organizations of the time, charged with tasks such as negotiating with the British, who controlled Palestine, and raising funds in the United States to support the push for statehood. David Ben-Gurion, who became Israel's first prime minister when Israel was established in 1948, later called her the "Jewish woman who got the money which made the state possible." Golda played such an important role that she was one of only two women who signed the Israeli Declaration of Independence.

Following independence, Ben-Gurion appointed Golda as Israel's minister to the Soviet Union, then a critical ally, and she traveled to Moscow armed with the first Israeli-issued passport. She was then elected to the Knesset, the Israeli parliament, and served as minister of labor, a position she loved. In 1956, she was named minister of foreign affairs, the second-highest position in the Israeli government. At the time, she was the only female foreign minister in the world. Since she was now Israel's chief diplomatic representative, she was asked to choose a Hebrew surname; she selected Meir, which means "illumination."

In 1966, Golda felt that her mission was accomplished and retired from the government to spend more time with her children and grandchildren. But following the sudden death of Prime Minister Levi Eshkol in 1969, she was asked to become Israel's fourth prime minister because she was considered the person who had the necessary stature and experience needed to lead the nation. At the time, she was only the third woman in the modern world to serve as a nation's prime minister. She led the country through the 1973 Yom Kippur War, a surprise attack by Arab states against Israel. In 1974, the year she stepped down as prime minster, a Gallup poll named her the most admired woman of the year in the United States.

Known as "the Iron Lady of Israeli politics" and Israel's "Lioness," Golda never wavered from her goal of establishing a strong Jewish state. Her toughness and grit were legendary: upon her death, it was revealed that she had been secretly ill with leukemia for twelve years.

TODAY: Since Golda, no woman has served as prime minister of Israel and only a few have held important cabinet posts. Although the numbers remain small compared to men, there has been a steady increase in the number of women serving in the Knesset—the Israeli parliament.

GERTRUDE BERG

Radio and Television Star
Who Built a Media Empire

1899–1966

BIRTHPLACE: East Harlem, New York City
BIRTHDATE: October 3, 1899

GERTRUDE BERG, OR TILLIE, AS SHE WAS NAMED AT BIRTH, SPENT HER SUMMERS AT HER FATHER'S JEWISH RESORT HOTEL IN THE BORSCHT BELT IN NEW YORK'S CATSKILL MOUNTAINS. There, she delighted in creating, producing, and performing in comic sketches for guests on rainy days. She loved making up characters and imitating accents.

Radio, then a new and exciting technology, was just coming into its own, connecting people in their homes with live news and entertainment for the first time. Tillie set her sights on making it big in radio drama, and after high school, she took night classes in playwriting at

Columbia University. A decade or so after getting married and having two children, she changed her name to Gertrude and began writing radio scripts.

In 1929, Gertrude approached NBC executives with a sample script for a show she called *The Rise of the Goldbergs,* based on a character she invented named Molly Goldberg, a bighearted gossipy Jewish mother who spoke with a thick Yiddish accent and was the matriarch of an immigrant family living in a tenement in a poor New York City neighborhood in the Bronx. Since the script was handwritten in pencil and hard to read, Gertrude read it aloud, voicing all the characters. Wowed, the network took a chance on what would become one of the longest-running daily shows in the golden age of radio.

Gertrude was a hard worker, and every morning she woke up early to write the day's script, then produced the show and starred in the role of Molly. Her husband typed the scripts. At the show's peak, Gertrude's character of Molly Goldberg was voted the second-most-admired woman in America, after First Lady Eleanor Roosevelt. Gertrude then adapted the show for Broadway, and in 1949, she persuaded CBS to let her bring the show, now called *The Goldbergs,* to the new medium of television.

The Goldbergs was an immediate hit on TV. Its humorous and warm portrayal of the American immigrant experience spoke directly to newcomers arriving in the United States from all over the world. It was also the first sitcom, or situation comedy, about a Jewish family, making it many Americans' introduction to Jewish holidays such as Passover and traditional Jewish foods such as borscht and matzoh. In 1950, the show's first year, Gertrude won television's first Emmy Award for lead actress in a comedy series.

Molly Goldberg was so beloved that people often forgot she was a fictional character. But behind Molly was the talented Gertrude, who lived with her family in a luxurious apartment on Park Avenue in Manhattan and didn't speak with a Yiddish accent. Gertrude was also a savvy businesswoman; she is one of the few writers, producers, and stars, let alone women, who maintained ownership and creative control over her work in American broadcasting history.

Gertrude loved her work, and when *The Goldbergs* went off the air in 1956, she moved on to new challenges. She starred in a new television series, won a Tony Award for a performance in the Broadway play *A Majority of One* in 1959, wrote bestselling books, and much more. Strangely, while many of the television episodes of *The*

Goldbergs have survived, Gertrude's groundbreaking multimedia career and her alter ego Molly Goldberg, once the most famous fictional Jewish woman in America, have largely been forgotten.

TODAY: Other famous women such as Lucille Ball, Martha Stewart, and Oprah Winfrey followed in Gertrude's footsteps to build media empires. While the top echelons of the entertainment industry remain male-dominated, women continue to make significant inroads.

TWENTIETH CENTURY

AMERICAN WOMEN GAINED THE RIGHT TO VOTE IN FEDERAL ELECTIONS IN 1920, JUST THIRTEEN YEARS BEFORE RBG WAS BORN. The seventy-year struggle for women's suffrage had ended in victory, but many inequities remained. RBG greatly admired the women who led the charge of "second wave" feminism to confront these inequities in all fields. She had the opportunity to meet some of them, such as the Nobel Prize–winning scientist Rita Levi-Montalcini; and the first woman to own a seat on the New York Stock Exchange, Muriel Siebert. Others she admired from afar. RBG called Bessie Margolin, who fought for equal pay for women, "remarkable," and she was a passionate fan of the opera singer Roberta Peters.

Gender discrimination was far from the only prejudice challenging humanity in the first half of the twentieth century. World War I and World War II killed millions of people, and in the latter, European Jews in particular were murdered en masse by the Nazis. Two of the women in this chapter were sent to Nazi death camps because they were Jews: Regina Jonas and Anne Frank, from whose diary RBG said she drew strength. Neither survived. Some of our other brave and brilliant women were more fortunate; they either successfully hid from the Nazis or lived elsewhere. But wherever they lived, many of them encountered anti-Semitism as well as gender discrimination.

REGINA JONAS

First Ordained Female
Rabbi in Jewish History

1902–1944

BIRTHPLACE: *Berlin, Germany*
BIRTHDATE: *August 3, 1902*

AS A GIRL IN BERLIN, GERMANY, REGINA JONAS LOVED STUDYING JEWISH HISTORY, HEBREW, AND THE TORAH. Her classmates in high school recalled that even at a young age, Regina talked about becoming a rabbi. She knew that a woman had never been ordained, but she was determined to change the status quo.

Her parents were poor but did what they could to help her achieve her dream. Regina also found several Orthodox rabbis to study with, including one who was known for supporting religious education for girls. He recognized her passion for Judaism and her talent and met with her weekly to study Talmud and discuss rabbinical texts.

Regina attended a teachers' seminary where she was trained to teach Judaism to girls, but that wasn't enough for her. When she was twenty-two, she enrolled in one of the few Jewish schools in Germany that admitted women. The rest of her female classmates planned to be teachers, but Regina didn't hide the fact that she wanted to be a rabbi. In the thesis she submitted in 1930, she laid out the first known attempt at a halachic or Jewish legal argument for why Orthodox Jews should establish a female rabbinate as a logical extension of Jewish tradition. She wrote, among other things, that female rabbis were a "cultural necessity" because of "female qualities" such as compassion and psychological intuition. At the end she concluded: "Almost nothing halachically but prejudice and lack of familiarity stand against women holding rabbinic office."

A shift away from strict tradition was occurring within Germany's Orthodox Jewish community at the time, but ordaining a woman was still considered out of bounds. The school continued to refuse her request for ordination, but Regina didn't give up. In 1935, nearly five years after she graduated, she was ordained by an important liberal rabbi. Finding a position as a rabbi, however, was a challenge. Although known as a "thinking and agile preacher," no Berlin synagogue would hire her. Instead she found work providing pastoral care in the city's hospitals and other social institutions.

That same year, the situation for German Jews gravely deteriorated with the introduction of the infamous Nuremberg Race Laws, which institutionalized Nazi racial theories. Jews were stripped of their citizenship and other rights, and many of Berlin's rabbis were imprisoned or emigrated. Regina stayed on, filling in for them, preaching at weekday afternoon synagogue services, and caring for the elderly, whose economic situation became desperate after the destruction of Jewish businesses, synagogues, and homes from November 9 to 10, 1938, known as Kristallnacht.

"If I confess what motivated me, a woman, to become a rabbi, two things come to mind," Regina wrote at the time. "My belief in God's calling and my love of humans. God planted in our heart skills and a vocation without asking about gender. Therefore, it is the duty of men and women alike to work and create according to the skills given by God."

When Berlin's Jews, including herself, were forced to work in factories and were no longer able to attend synagogue, she led uplifting special services for them. When Regina and her mother were deported to the Theresienstadt concentration camp in German-occupied

Czechoslovakia in 1942, she continued to preach and render spiritual care to her fellow inmates.

In 1944, she was sent to Auschwitz and killed. Her amazing journey and work was then forgotten by history until a scholar discovered her papers in an obscure East Berlin archive in the early 1990s, a few years after the wall separating the communist part of the city from West Berlin came down. Until then, most people believed the first female rabbi to be Sally Priesand, who was ordained by the Reform movement in the United States in 1972.

Regina would be thrilled to know that today all Jewish denominations except the Orthodox ordain women as rabbis, and that even many modern Orthodox rabbis now embrace the ideas she put forth in her 1930 thesis. While they are not called rabbis, modern Orthodox women can now be ordained as *maharats*—female leaders of Jewish law, spirituality, and Torah.

TODAY: *Since 1972, more than a thousand women have been ordained as rabbis around the world and they have transformed the Jewish world with their scholarship, teaching, preaching, and leadership.*

RITA LEVI-MONTALCINI

*Neurobiologist Who Won
the Nobel Prize in Medicine*

1909–2012

BIRTHPLACE: *Turin, Italy*
BIRTHDATE: *April 22, 1909*

*RITA LEVI-MONTALCINI WAS BORN IN TURIN, A CITY IN
NORTHERN ITALY, INTO A HIGHLY CULTURED SEPHARDI
JEWISH FAMILY.* Her father was an electrical engineer
and mathematician, her mother a painter. After a family
friend died of cancer, Rita was inspired to become a doctor. But although her father had great respect for women,
he also held traditional patriarchal values and decided
that Rita and her two sisters should not attend university
or pursue professional careers because it would interfere
with their duties as wives and mothers. Their brother,
however, could choose his own path.

But Rita was determined to go to medical school,
and her father, although hesitant, eventually agreed. She

studied medicine and surgery at the University of Turin, and in 1936 she graduated first in her class. She then enrolled in advanced neurology and psychiatry courses and investigated nervous system cells as an assistant to one of her professors. Rita loved her research, but in 1938 her work was interrupted by world events. She was forced to leave the university—and her laboratory—when Italian dictator Benito Mussolini issued a law barring Jews from academic and professional careers.

Rita refused to let the new law interrupt her research. She set up a laboratory in her bedroom to study the nerve cells of chicken embryos. She didn't have any tools, so she fashioned tiny scalpels from sewing needles and used a watchmaker's forceps. Nor was she deterred when Allied bombing forced the family to flee the city; she rebuilt her lab in the countryside. She even continued her work when Nazi Germany invaded Italy in September 1943 and authorities began to round up Jews. While she and her family lived in hiding in Florence, Rita reassembled her lab and resumed her work.

Rita and her family were lucky. They survived. Upon Italy's liberation in 1944, they came out of hiding, and Rita worked for the first time as a physician, treating patients suffering from typhus and other deadly diseases in a refugee camp. When the war ended, she was able to return to her university position.

Rita's chicken embryo research led to a job at Washington University in St. Louis, Missouri, where she and another doctor, Stanley Cohen, would detect a protein in embryos that unlocked the mystery of how nerve cells grow. It was a big breakthrough that transformed the study of cell development and advanced the understanding and treatment of cancer and serious neurological disorders such as Alzheimer's. The discovery earned them the Nobel Prize in Physiology or Medicine in 1986.

After thirty years at Washington University, Rita returned to Italy. Rather than retire, she established the Institute of Cell Biology in Rome, the European Brain Research Institute, and the Rita Levi-Montalcini Foundation to educate girls and women in Africa. She also was named a senator for life, one of Italy's highest honors. The woman once barred from studying and working in her own country became a celebrated figure. When Rita died at age 103 in Rome, the city's mayor called her death a loss "for all of humanity."

TODAY: Since the first Nobel Prizes were awarded in 1901, only 3 percent have been given to women.

BESSIE MARGOLIN

*Pioneering Lawyer for Equal Rights
and Equal Pay for Women*

1909–1996

BIRTHPLACE: *Brownsville neighborhood of Brooklyn,
New York*
BIRTHDATE: *1909*

*WHEN BESSIE MARGOLIN WAS FOUR, HER MOTHER DIED
AND HER FATHER SENT HER TO LIVE IN A JEWISH ORPHAN-
AGE IN NEW ORLEANS, LOUISIANA.* This could have been
a terrible experience, but it wasn't. The orphanage was
well run and provided her with an excellent education.
In fact, Bessie was such a good student that she went on
to college and then became the only female student at
Tulane University's law school. She even won a prestigious fellowship to Yale, where she earned her doctorate
degree in law.

By then, she was eager to find a job. But the year was

1933, and only 2 percent of lawyers at the time were women. Bessie had written a brilliant legal analysis of laws affecting company reorganizations that appeared in *The Yale Law Journal* with just her initials. Inquiries from law firms had followed, but when recruiters discovered those initials belonged to a woman, they lost interest.

Only one employer was receptive to hiring female attorneys: the federal government. That's why Bessie went to work, first for the Tennessee Valley Authority—one of President Franklin Delano Roosevelt's New Deal programs to develop a region hit hard by the Great Depression—and then in 1939 for the Department of Labor in Washington, DC.

Even at the Department of Labor, Bessie constantly ran up against gender discrimination in the workplace. In 1942, she became frustrated when male lawyers in the Labor Department were given promotions and she wasn't. She wrote a letter stating her case to Secretary of Labor Frances Perkins, herself the first woman to hold a position in an American president's cabinet. Bessie got her promotion.

She used her new position to fight for equal pay for women. By the time Congress passed the Equal Pay Act in 1963—which amended the 1938 Fair Labor Standards

Act to make gender discrimination in pay illegal—Bessie had filed three hundred equal-pay lawsuits in forty states on behalf of eighteen thousand female employees. Once the act was in place, she became responsible for its enforcement.

During her career, Bessie argued twenty-four cases before the U.S. Supreme Court, winning all but three. She was a forceful champion for the Fair Labor Stan dards Act, which established the U.S. minimum wage, regulated overtime pay, and restricted child labor. When she retired from the Labor Department after thirty-three years, Supreme Court Chief Justice Earl Warren praised her for developing "the flesh and sinews" around the "bare bones" of the law.

Bessie never forgot that she was Jewish and that her parents had fled religious persecution in Russia. After World War II, she took a special six-month assignment in Nuremberg, Germany. There she helped draft the rules establishing the American military tribunals that meted out justice to accused major Nazi war criminals.

Interestingly, Bessie didn't initially think of herself as a feminist but became one through her work, joining the National Organization for Women (NOW) as a founding member in 1966.

TODAY: *Despite Bessie's efforts and more recent laws such as the Lilly Ledbetter Fair Pay Act of 2009, women are paid significantly less than men. The wage gap, however, is narrowing.*

BELLA ABZUG

*Lawyer and Congresswoman with
a Bold Voice for Women's Rights*

1920–1998

BIRTHPLACE: *New York, New York*
BIRTHDATE: *July 24, 1920*

AS A CHILD, BELLA ABZUG WAS VERY CLOSE TO HER
GRANDFATHER AND OFTEN ACCOMPANIED HIM TO
SERVICES AT HIS NEW YORK ORTHODOX SYNAGOGUE.
She had a beautiful voice and knew all the Hebrew prayers
by heart—and he enjoyed showing off her talents to his
friends. But from a young age, it bothered her that girls
and women were consigned to the balcony and that she
wasn't allowed to sit next to him in the main sanctuary.
Her sense of injustice grew when her father died when
she was thirteen. Since he didn't have any sons, Bella
refused to conform to tradition, and boldly attended
synagogue every day for eleven months to say Kaddish,

the mourner's prayer, for him. Because she was female, she was not permitted to join the men in reciting the Kaddish, so she stood and prayed alone.

These early experiences turned Bella into a staunch feminist and inspired her to become a lawyer to fight for women's equality. It was unusual for women to become lawyers in the 1940s, and although she was a top student and the president of both her high school and college classes, Harvard Law School refused to admit her. So she went to Columbia Law School, and eventually opened her own law practice, bravely tackling injustices of all kinds, such as labor and tenants' rights and civil rights.

Bella was known for her outsized personality, booming voice, and big hats, and she was impossible to ignore, a very useful attribute in politics. In 1970, she ran for the U.S. Congress with the campaign slogan: "This woman's place is in the House—the House of Representatives." She won and became the first Jewish congresswoman since Florence Prag Kahn, and the first female Jewish Democrat. Once in Washington, she poured her prodigious determination into fighting for equal rights for women. In 1971, Bella helped shepherd the Equal Rights Amendment (ERA) through the House of Representatives. The proposed amendment to the U.S. Constitution prohibited discrimination on the basis of sex. (It was later approved by the Senate but is not part of the Constitution because thirty-eight states did not ratify it before the deadlines set by Congress.) She addressed other inequities as well, drafting what became a law that finally allowed women to obtain credit cards and loans in their own names. To encourage women to run for political office and to provide funds for their campaigns, she helped establish the National Women's Political Caucus.

She gave up her seat in 1976 to run for the Senate, which at that time did not have any women in it. She lost by less than 1 percent. She never served in political office again, but Bella, the daughter of poor Russian immigrants, remained a high-profile figure for the rest of her life, fighting for the rights of downtrodden Americans, whatever their race, creed, or gender. She was so fierce a champion for these causes that her nickname was "Battling Bella."

TODAY: Bella remains a legendary figure among feminists, and in 2017 was named by Time magazine as one of its "50 Women Who Made American Political History."

ROSALIND FRANKLIN

*Ingenious Biophysicist Who
Discovered the Structure of DNA*

1920–1958

BIRTHPLACE: *Notting Hill, London, England*
BIRTHDATE: *July 25, 1920*

ROSALIND FRANKLIN EXCELLED AT SCIENCE AND ATTENDED ONE OF THE FEW GIRLS' SCHOOLS IN LONDON THAT TAUGHT PHYSICS AND CHEMISTRY. By age fifteen, she knew she wanted to be a scientist. Her father, a wealthy London banker and teacher, discouraged her—not because he didn't believe in her ability, but because he knew how difficult it was for women to establish themselves in the scientific world. Rosalind was determined, however, and earned a doctorate in chemistry at Cambridge University. Unfortunately, she quickly discovered that her father was right; despite the fact that she had won prestigious fellowships and published groundbreaking papers, both Rosalind and her work would often be deliberately overlooked by her male colleagues.

Nowhere was this as obvious as in 1953 when scientists James Watson and Francis Crick published their famous article, "Molecular Structure of Nucleic Acids." The paper described the double helix structure of DNA, one of the most important biological discoveries of the twentieth century. Although the men's findings were based on Rosalind's study of DNA through X-ray crystallography, her name was mentioned only in passing at the very end of the paper. Two of her male colleagues, including her collaborator Maurice Wilkins, had shared her work with Watson and Crick without her permission. That disclosure had allowed Watson and Crick to build the chemical model of the DNA molecule and to calculate the size and structure of the helix.

In the face of unrelenting discrimination, Franklin forged ahead with her work, conducting other successful investigations. She used the X-ray crystallography techniques she developed to examine the structure of RNA, which contains the genetic information of many viruses. She did fruitful work on plant and animal viruses, including polio, an infectious disease that killed and paralyzed more than half a million people worldwide each year during the 1940s and 1950s.

Rosalind once wrote that being a woman was not her only problem. She felt out of place in British scientific institutions where few Jews or foreigners worked. Fate was also not kind to Rosalind. She died of ovarian cancer at age thirty-seven. But she never doubted that she had chosen the right path. The inscription she composed for her gravestone reads: *Her Research and Discoveries on Viruses Remain of Lasting Benefit to Mankind.*

When the Nobel committee awarded the 1962 Prize in Physiology or Medicine to Watson, Crick, and Wilkins for solving the structure of DNA, one name was missing: Rosalind Franklin. Although few today would dispute that she deserved the recognition, the Nobel Prize is awarded only to scientists during their lives, never afterward. Nevertheless, many articles and books have been written about her, and her achievements are far better known now than they were during her lifetime.

TODAY: A 2018 Pew Research Center report found that half of American women working in science, technology, engineering, and math (STEM) jobs said they experienced discrimination at work due to their gender.

BETTY FRIEDAN

Author and Organizer Who Led the Fight for "Women's Liberation"

1921–2006

BIRTHPLACE: *Peoria, Illinois*
BIRTHDATE: *February 4, 1921*

BETTY FRIEDAN'S CHILDHOOD IN PEORIA, ILLINOIS, WASN'T A HAPPY ONE. She wasn't poor. Her father was a Russian immigrant who had found success in the jewelry business. But her mother was not content. She had quit her job as society writer for the local newspaper at her husband's insistence and felt confined as a housewife. With her own ambitions unfulfilled, she was often critical of Betty, who, while smart and intellectual, was rebellious. Betty was determined not to make the same mistake as her mother.

In high school, Betty was denied admission to a sorority because she was Jewish. She found other outlets, becoming an editor of the school newspaper and founding a literary magazine. She then did well at Smith College, majoring in psychology and graduating summa cum laude. She started graduate school in California, but when a boyfriend discouraged her from studying for her doctorate, she left him and took off for New York City to become a journalist.

There, Betty devoted herself to the pursuit of justice. Her "passion against injustice," she once said, originated from her feelings about "the injustice of anti-Semitism." She found a job at a union-oriented wire service and newspaper writing about injustices of all kinds. She got married and had a child and didn't quit her job. She seemed to have it all until she was fired when she became pregnant with the second of her three children. Suddenly Betty was a reluctant and restless full-time housewife just as her mother had been.

As her fifteenth college reunion approached, she wondered if her classmates felt the same way. So she surveyed them—and discovered that many of them did. Betty threw herself into studying what she called "the problem with no name." From that research came her groundbreaking 1963 book, *The Feminine Mystique,* which sold millions of copies and was translated into many of the world's languages. The book brought "second-wave" feminism to suburban American women four decades after the seventy-year struggle for women's suffrage had been won, and Betty became the voice of housewives who yearned for lives outside their homes.

Her quest for what was often called "women's liberation" was controversial. Some friends shunned her and her family. But Betty, an impassioned speaker, pushed ahead, calling for equal pay and equal opportunity for women in education and jobs, and for the end of work discrimination based on pregnancy. She wrote other books and cofounded the National Organization for Women (NOW), served as its first president, and organized a women's strike for equal rights. To encourage women to run for political office and to make sure they had money for their campaigns, she helped establish the National Women's Political Caucus.

Betty put her skills of persuasion to work to help propel the Equal Rights Amendment (ERA) through Congress to guarantee the same treatment for men and women under the law. It didn't become part of the Constitution, however, because thirty-eight states did not ratify it before the deadlines passed. Still, her books— and relentless activism—dramatically changed how many American women viewed themselves and chose to live their lives.

TODAY: *Nearly sixty years after <u>The Feminine Mystique</u> was published, the book is still studied in courses on feminism and continues to spark discussion and controversy.*

NADINE GORDIMER

*Nobel Prize–Winning Writer
and Activist for Human Rights
in South Africa*

1923–2014

BIRTHPLACE: *Springs, Transvaal, South Africa*
BIRTHDATE: *November 20, 1923*

NADINE GORDIMER GREW UP IN A GOLD MINING TOWN NEAR JOHANNESBURG IN SOUTH AFRICA. As a schoolgirl she was warned to stay away from the compounds where the Black mine workers lived, separate from the town's white residents. But from a young age Nadine was appalled by the way the country's white minority treated its majority Black population.

Her parents were white, middle-class secular Jewish immigrants. Her father ran a jewelry store and had been raised as an observant Orthodox Jew in Latvia. Her mother, a housewife, was from a well-established Jewish family in England. They were newcomers to South Africa and they didn't speak out against the rise of racial oppression, which eventually led to apartheid, the country's system of white-minority domination of Blacks.

Nadine began to write at age nine and her first story was published when she was fourteen. As a young adult, she spent a year at a university in Johannesburg. For the first time, she was exposed to life in one of the Black townships, Sophiatown. After leaving school to become a full-time writer, she joined the African National Congress, the main group leading the struggle against apartheid. She remained a secret member even after the organization was outlawed by the South African government. She helped its leader, Nelson Mandela, compose his famous statement of defiance at the trial where he was sentenced to life imprisonment for opposing the regime.

While she did not set out to write political novels, she grounded her stories in the injustices of the apartheid system and the police state it fostered. She was known for her sensitive portrayals of individuals living amid the complexities of South African society, from poor Black villagers and house servants to wealthy white aristocrats and government officials. Nadine published thirteen novels, as well as short stories and many works of nonfiction. The South African government banned some of her books, but her work was read around the world and brought attention to the atrocities happening to Black South Africans under apartheid. In 1991, she became the first South African to win the Nobel Prize for Literature.

Nadine believed that the key to a meaningful life was honesty and integrity and that writers had a responsibility as human beings to take a stand for what is right. Although she called herself a "Jew forever," she insisted that her support for Black people in South Africa had nothing to do with being Jewish. "Social conscience does not come from being part of a persecuted race," she said.

After the collapse of apartheid and the advent of Black majority rule in South Africa in 1994, Nadine celebrated the election of Mandela to the presidency. She continued to write about the impact of racism and economic inequality on both white and Black people, and spoke out against human rights injustices perpetrated under Black majority rule. Nadine never stopped standing for—and writing about—the causes she believed in.

TODAY: Nadine's books are still read throughout the world, but she is better known for her political activism against apartheid and on behalf of other causes, such as raising money to fight HIV/AIDS, one of the global pandemics of her time.

MURIEL FAYE SIEBERT

*Wall Street Maverick and First Woman
on the New York Stock Exchange*

1928–2013

BIRTHPLACE: Cleveland, Ohio
BIRTHDATE: September 12, 1928

*MURIEL FAYE SIEBERT— "MICKIE," AS SHE WAS KNOWN—
GREW UP IN CLEVELAND, OHIO.* She studied accounting
in college and was the only woman in her money and
banking class. But when her father fell ill and her family
could no longer afford the tuition, she was forced to leave
school. After he died, she drove to New York City determined to succeed in the financial capital of the world. All
she had was a used car and five hundred dollars.

Finding a job was tough. She suspected that her
female name sent her résumé directly into the trash
bin. Only when she began to use her initials, M.F., did
finance firms want to meet her. Once she was in the door,

interviewers recognized her intelligence and ability, and she secured a series of research and analysis jobs at brokerage houses. But she found the same barriers at every firm—significantly lower salaries for women than men, assignments to accounts men didn't want, and industry clubs closed to women.

She also encountered anti-Semitism. Colleagues sometimes made derogatory jokes and remarks about Jews. According to one story, she occasionally sent them a note after they made such comments at lunch: *Roses are red, violets are bluish, in case you didn't know it, I'm Jewish. I enjoyed lunch, Mickie.*

In 1967, she decided to remedy the situation by opening her own brokerage firm, Muriel Siebert & Co., Inc., and taking the bold step of buying a seat on the New York Stock Exchange (NYSE) so that she could buy and sell stocks for herself and others without an intermediary. This last was easier said than done, because the stock exchange was an exclusively male "club." At least one member had to sponsor her and the first nine men she asked refused. But the tenth said yes and Muriel made history. At the time she bought her seat, all 1,365 other members of the NYSE were men.

It took ten years for another woman to gain entry and twenty years for the NYSE to put a women's restroom outside the seventh-floor club room where deals were made. And that happened only after Muriel threatened to install a Porta-Potty there.

Throughout her career, Muriel championed women and minorities because she believed that hiring women and minorities made companies stronger. She thought everyone needed to understand how to use money well and developed a program to teach essential financial skills to New York City middle and high school students, as well as adults.

She also gave back; her company shared its profits generously with charities. And she put her knowledge to work for the public; during her five-year tenure as the first woman to serve as New York State's superintendent of banks, not a single bank failed. In 2002, she wrote an autobiography, *Changing the Rules: Adventures of a Wall Street Maverick.*

When Muriel died, the New York Stock Exchange named a room for her, Siebert Hall, in recognition of her pioneering role in opening the field of finance to women. The first room named for an individual at the NYSE, it features memorabilia from Muriel's groundbreaking career.

TODAY: *While more women work in finance, there are still far too few in the top echelons of investment and banking. Only a small fraction of senior management positions in venture capital, private equity, and hedge fund firms are held by women.*

ANNE FRANK

Young Writer Who Kept an Inspirational Diary While Hiding from the Nazis

1929–1945

BIRTHPLACE: *Frankfurt, Germany*
BIRTHDATE: *June 12, 1929*

ANNE WAS FOUR YEARS OLD WHEN THE NAZIS SEIZED POWER IN GERMANY IN 1933. Recognizing that the Nazis, led by Adolf Hitler, were dangerous, her parents left their home in Frankfurt, Germany, and fled to the Netherlands with Anne and her older sister, Margot.

The family settled in Amsterdam, and for some years they were safe there. But in 1942, Nazi forces conquered the Netherlands and authorities began rounding up Dutch Jews for deportation to Nazi concentration camps in German-occupied Poland. Anne's father, Otto, found a hiding place for them, an attic in the warehouse he rented for his business that they called the Secret Annex.

A bookcase hid the entrance and only four trusted people, including Otto's secretary, knew where the family and another four people were concealed. They brought Anne and the others food and news of the war daily.

Anne chronicled her thoughts in a red-and-white checked cloth-covered diary her parents had given her for her thirteenth birthday. She called the diary Kitty, and all her entries began, *Dear Kitty.* She wrote of her ambition to become a writer, perhaps not realizing that she already was one. Her prose was clear and she took time to edit and polish her sentences to make them beautiful. In her diary, she examined her feelings, both positive and negative, and pondered human nature. Despite what was happening outside the attic, she was convinced that people were basically good, and that good was a force more powerful than evil.

Anne was also a feminist. In one of the last entries in her diary, she wrote about the "great injustice" in the false assumption that women were inferior to men. "Until recently, women silently went along with this, which was stupid, since the longer it's kept up, the more deeply entrenched it becomes." She was heartened that education had opened women's eyes and that both women and men now recognized "how wrong it was to tolerate this state of affairs for so long."

In August 1944, just two months after Anne's fifteenth birthday, Nazi soldiers discovered the Secret Annex. All but Anne and Margot were deported to the Auschwitz-Birkenau concentration camp in Poland. The sisters were sent to the Bergen-Belsen camp in northern Germany. Both girls died of typhus during the winter of 1945, just a few months before the camp's liberation.

Anne's father was the only survivor from the group that had hidden in the Secret Annex. Anne's diary, which Otto's secretary had found and saved, also survived. Otto arranged for its publication in Dutch in June 1947, two weeks after what would have been Anne's eighteenth birthday. This first edition of *The Diary of a Young Girl* by Anne Frank sold about three thousand copies, but thanks to Otto's persistence, it was also published in Germany, France, and the United States and became a bestseller. It has now been translated into more than seventy languages and has sold more than thirty million copies.

Anne's writing has educated young people—and adults—around the world about the Holocaust and how cruelty and race-based hatred overwhelmed human goodness in her time. Her youthful honesty, intellect, humor, and resilience continue to inspire new readers.

TODAY: In 1960, the Frank family's hiding place in Amsterdam was transformed into a museum, the Anne Frank House, which receives many visitors every year. But the dangerous forces that cut short Anne's life have not disappeared: racial hatred, anti-Semitism, and even denial that the Holocaust happened persist.

ROBERTA PETERS

American Soprano Who
Became a Star and Popularized
Opera in the United States

1930–2017

BIRTHPLACE: *The Bronx, New York City*
BIRTHDATE: *May 4, 1930*

ROBERTA PETERS LOVED TO SING AND HER PARENTS, A NEW YORK HATMAKER AND A SHOE SALESMAN, COULD TELL THAT SHE HAD A FABULOUS VOICE. Despite their modest means, they encouraged her to pursue a career in music and made sure that she had everything she needed. Her mother told her, "One day if you work hard, you'll make the Met," referring to the famous Metropolitan Opera House in Manhattan.

Roberta's first break came when her grandfather, the head waiter at a famous Jewish summer resort in the Catskill Mountains, convinced Jan Peerce, a famous opera tenor and cantor, to listen to his twelve-year-old granddaughter sing. Impressed, Peerce sent Roberta to study with his voice teacher, William Herman.

Training to be an opera star was an all-consuming task. Roberta studied with Herman six days a week for six years, leaving school after junior high. A stern teacher, he demanded that Roberta learn all about opera, not just its music. He taught her self-discipline and the importance of staying in top physical shape. She learned poise and how to strengthen her diaphragm for breath control, and studied Italian, French, German, piano, drama, and ballet.

Her tenacity was rewarded when she auditioned for the Met. Its general manager was captivated by the power of the young coloratura soprano's voice. He planned her Met debut for February 1951, when she would sing the Queen of the Night in Mozart's *The Magic Flute*.

Instead, on November 17, 1950, the general manager called Roberta to the Met to sing the role of Zerlina in *Don Giovanni* when the singer cast in that role fell ill. Roberta knew the part from her studies with Herman. With just six hours to prepare, she and her parents took the subway from their apartment in the Bronx. When they reached the opera house, Roberta, who had never performed in public before, had just enough time for costume fittings and introductions to the other singers and the orchestra conductor. The regular cast members guided her to where she needed to be onstage throughout the performance.

She was a sensation. Six years of rigorous training had made Roberta an overnight opera star. She remained a Met star for thirty-five years, singing 515 performances in more than twenty roles, enchanting audiences in parts such as the Queen of the Night, Rosina in Rossini's *The Barber of Seville,* and Gilda in Verdi's *Rigoletto.*

In addition to having the longest tenure of any soprano at the Met, Roberta appeared on radio and television shows, as well as in TV commercials and movies. Funny and smart, she was a frequent guest on the major television variety shows of the twentieth century, appearing sixty-five times on the highly popular *Ed Sullivan Show.* Through these appearances she introduced millions of people to opera.

Roberta was proud of her heritage. Although she had no formal Jewish education, she had attended an Orthodox synagogue with her grandmother, from whom she learned Yiddish. She delighted in singing her favorite Yiddish folk tunes to Jewish audiences and was devoted to Israel, to which she traveled often. In 1967 in Israel, while she was onstage performing with the famous tenor Richard Tucker, war broke out between Israel and some of its hostile neighbors. She and Tucker were urged to leave but insisted on staying and singing to show their support.

TODAY: Although women have performed in operas throughout history, a recent survey reveals relatively few women in composer, librettist, and managerial roles. In 2016 the Met presented L'Amour de Loin, by Kaija Saariaho, its first opera written by a woman since 1903.

JUDY RESNIK

*Astronaut and First Jewish
Woman to Travel to Space*

1949–1986

BIRTHPLACE: *Akron, Ohio*
BIRTHDATE: *April 5, 1949*

*JUDY RESNICK WAS BORN TWENTY YEARS BEFORE
AMERICAN ASTRONAUTS NEIL ARMSTRONG AND BUZZ
ALDRIN BECAME THE FIRST HUMANS TO LAND ON THE
MOON.* In fact, when she was a child, there was no such
job as astronaut, and NASA, the U.S. space agency,
hadn't yet been established. So it is no surprise that growing up in Akron, Ohio, Judy never imagined she might
one day travel to space.

She was, however, very interested in Judaism. Her
parents, immigrants from Kyiv, were active in Jewish
causes, and the family's home was an observant one.
She was particularly close to her father, a multilingual

optometrist and yeshiva-trained cantor. She attended Hebrew school and became a bat mitzvah, which was rare for girls of her time.

Judy excelled in school, especially in math and science. But her great passion was music. A gifted musician, she dreamed of a career as a concert pianist and hoped one day to attend the Juilliard School, a prestigious performing arts school, in New York City.

After graduating at the top of her high school class and earning a perfect score on her SAT (she was one of only sixteen women in the history of the United States to do so at the time), she changed direction. Although she had been accepted at Juilliard, she headed to Carnegie Tech (now Carnegie Mellon University) in Pittsburgh to study electrical engineering.

She loved engineering and went on to graduate school. While studying for her doctorate, Judy designed missile and radar projects for the military. She also conducted research as a biomedical engineer and qualified as a professional aircraft pilot.

In 1977, after years of barring women from the space program, NASA began recruiting women and minorities. Judy applied and a year later became one of the first six women accepted. She was then twenty-eight. She went through rigorous astronaut training and became a specialist in operating a remote-control mechanical arm that could move objects outside a spacecraft. During her first space flight on the shuttle *Discovery* in 1984, she unfurled a 102-foot-long solar sail, used to capture the sun's energy.

Judy was the second American woman to fly in space and the fourth worldwide. She was the first American Jewish astronaut, and only the second Jew to go into space—the first was a Soviet astronaut, Boris Volynov.

Her second flight into space launched on the morning of January 28, 1986. Millions watched on live TV as Judy and her six crewmates boarded the space shuttle *Challenger*. Judy planned to photograph Halley's comet during the journey. Catastrophe struck, as America watched, horrified; the shuttle exploded seventy-three seconds after taking off, killing everyone on board. It remains one of the worst space tragedies in history. Judy was only thirty-six years old. In her short life, she had traveled farther and accomplished more than she had ever imagined growing up—and more than most people even dream of.

TODAY: Only about 12 percent of the people who have traveled into space have been women. In 2020, NASA announced plans to put the first woman on the moon by 2024.

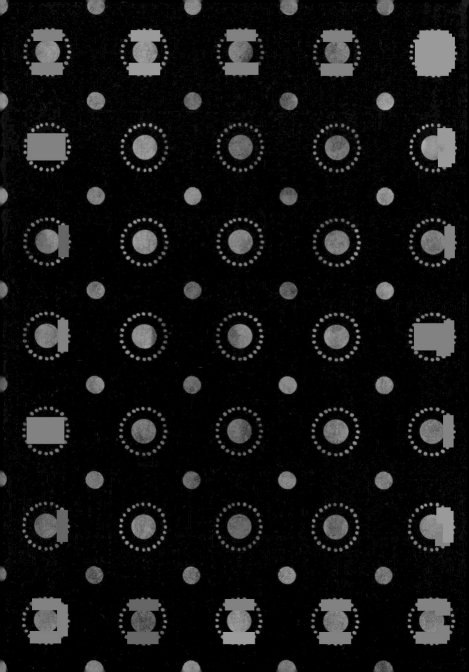

A CALL TO ACTION

Now that you've read about these brave and brilliant women, you know more about how long and hard the journey has been for women—Jewish and otherwise—to achieve the opportunities and rights they have today.

But the quest for equality is not over. True, women have made huge strides. In the Jewish world, girls now study the Torah and the Talmud, and in most denominations they can become a bat mitzvah. Jewish women are now spiritual, scholarly, artistic, and communal leaders. But there are still plenty of "glass ceilings" to break: women have yet to hold many of the highest-level positions in major Jewish organizations and are still paid significantly less than men for the same work. Women all across the United States face these same disparities. More doors are open, but unequal pay persists—despite the Equal Pay Act and other laws that have been passed.

Clearly, there is still a lot more work to do, legal and otherwise. Some people argue that women now have sufficient protection from discrimination because of the way courts and judges (including RBG) have interpreted the

Fourteenth Amendment. Others say we need a specific clause in the U.S. Constitution that more clearly spells out the guarantee of equal legal rights for all American citizens regardless of sex. Such an amendment, the Equal Rights Amendment (ERA), was first proposed in 1923, three years after women won the right to vote. It said simply: "Equality of rights under the law shall not be denied or abridged by the United States or by any state on account of sex."

It wasn't until 1972 that a group of female lawmakers such as the fiery Bella Abzug pushed it through both the U.S. House of Representatives and the Senate. However, a sufficient number of states (38) did *not* approve the ERA before the deadline, and it failed to become part of the Constitution. Although a new effort to pass the ERA began in 2017, RBG believed that the better option is for Congress to start over. She felt strongly that a new and more up-to-date equal rights amendment should be passed. "Every constitution in the world written since the year 1950 . . . has the equivalent of an equal rights amendment, and we don't," she observed in 2020.

For this to happen—and to ensure that laws preventing discrimination against girls and women are not reversed—we need more women in positions of power in government and throughout society. Believe it or not, when it comes to political leadership, the United States lags far behind much of the world! Yes, we elected our first female vice president in 2020, but many nations, including Germany, New Zealand, and Taiwan have already had successful female prime ministers or presidents. (As you read earlier, Golda Meir served as Israel's first and so far only female prime minister more than fifty years ago.) Sweden, Rwanda, and Mexico are among the countries with more women in parliament than in the U.S. Congress.

But there are also many countries where women have much less political representation than in the United States, and where women possess far fewer rights than men. In Saudi Arabia, for example, women remain second-class citizens and were given the right to vote and be candidates in local elections only in 2015, although politics is still considered a "male domain." They gained the right to drive only in 2018 and until 2019 were universally treated as legal minors, requiring a male relative's approval for a range of personal decisions, such as working, obtaining family records, and applying for a passport. They still need male consent to marry and to live on their own, and cannot pass on citizenship to their children or provide consent for their children to marry. In other countries, such as Afghanistan and Pakistan, women are often discouraged from voting, and it can be outright dangerous for them to do so, even though they possess the right on paper.

Gender equality is not just important because it is fair. As RBG often said, having more women in power benefits everyone. She liked to quote her dear friend Sandra Day O'Connor, the first woman on the Supreme Court of the United States: "As women achieve power, the barriers will fall. As society sees what women can do, as women see what women can do, there will be more women out there doing things, and we'll all be better off for it." In other words, most women bring important qualities to leadership that can make the world a better place for everyone.

So whatever your gender and whatever your passions, it makes sense to work toward increasing the number of women in positions of power. Pay attention to what is going on in the country—and the world. Think about what you want to achieve and make a plan to do it. Think about what you want to say, formulate a clear "pitch," and use your voice to speak out. Find ways to take positive action and join forces with like-minded friends and family members and good organizations. Don't forget people who disagree with you. Talk with them (don't argue with them); find ways of connecting, and gradually win them over as allies. Never let emotions get in your way and don't give up. Be patient: expect plenty of obstacles and put in the hard work to overcome them.

And whatever else you do, VOTE!

RBG said this is one of the most important things young people can do when they are old enough. "It is not just a right," she said. "It is an obligation." And don't stop there. Encourage other people to vote too. While you are at it, encourage women you know to run for office . . . and run for office yourself someday.

Be brave. Be brilliant. Soon it will be up to you to lead the way to a more just society. It will be your responsibility to carry on with the journey RBG, the women in this book, and others like them began. Moving the world forward is no easy task, but as their stories prove, it does move! And remember: when the going gets tough, you have female role models to inspire you.

ACKNOWLEDGMENTS

This book was only possible because of my cherished friend and collaborator, Ruth Bader Ginsburg. Even as she carried out her responsibilities on the Supreme Court and battled cancer, she worked on this book, writing her section and helping to select the women to feature. She closely read the first draft of each biography and recommended alterations. I learned much from her critical eye and wise suggestions. I wish she were here to see the book she helped imagine in its finished form.

Justice Ginsburg's devoted staff at the Supreme Court was incredibly supportive throughout the process. I am especially grateful to Lauren Stanley, who ironed out numerous details and scanned pages filled with Justice Ginsburg's handwritten comments. Kimberly McKenzie and Cathy Vaughn kindly helped with arrangements over the years. I would also like to thank Jane and Jim Ginsburg and their families for their support.

I am fortunate to work with a team of brilliant colleagues at *Moment Magazine*. Eileen Lavine, Ann Lewis, Pat Lewis, and Amy E. Schwartz generously gave of their time to read several drafts and make invaluable suggestions. Sarah Breger, Lilly Gelman, Tanya George, and Debbie Sann. I owe thank-yous to Pam Janis, who gave her heart to this project, and to Liat Wasserman and Marilyn Cooper for research assistance. Ross Bishton, Lilly Gelman, and Ellen Wexler assisted with fact checking. Johnna Raskin, as always, stood by to help as needed.

Other readers included Aimee Ginsburg Bikel, Max Epstein, Linda Feldmann, Glenn Frankel, Rabbi Lauren Holtzblatt, Elissa Janis, Aviva Kempner, Francine Klagsbrun, Dena Mandel, Gloria Levitas, Letty Cottin Pogrebin, Eliana Rosenthal, Shayna Sann, Nina Totenberg, and Janice Weinman. I thank them for their insightful comments.

Joan Nathan, Jane Freidman, and Altie Karper led me to my wonderful editor, Beverly Horowitz, and her assistant, Rebecca Gudelis. Michelle Cunningham's expert design of the book inside and out, paired with Bee Johnson's beautiful portrait illustrations, resulted in a stunning package. Miriam Furst, Gail Ross, Nancy Rubin, and Gwen Zuares provided wise counsel, as did Suzanne Borden, Eileen Dzik, Linda Feldmann, Linda Gallanter, Kathryn Gandal, Sheila Reiss, Mary Schwartz, Diane Troderman, Brenda Yanni, Gwen

Zuares, and all the members of *Moment*'s brain trust and boards.

My talented sister Marcy Epstein designed and painstakingly crafted the Tzedek Collar which we gave to Justice Ginsburg on September 18, 2019, when she received our Moment Magazine Human Rights Award. Marcy is always there for me, as are Donald and Jeanne Epstein, Michael Epstein, Molly Boyle, and their families. As I worked on this book, my beloved father, Dr. Seymour Epstein—a physicist with a gorgeous tenor voice—lit up my days by singing to me, in person and via FaceTime. Sadly, he died a few weeks shy of age one hundred shortly before this book went to the printer. My late mother, Ruth Goldberg Epstein, encouraged my love of reading and let me take as many books from the library as I could carry, sometimes more than I could carry. An inspiring speaker, a creative thinker, and an extraordinary leader, she was president of nearly every organization she ever joined and touched many lives, always for the better. I was fortunate to have her as a role model.

Matt Wang, Noah Phillips, and my husband, John O'Leary, make every day special—and their love and support made it possible for me to dedicate the necessary long hours to this book and, on an ongoing basis, to *Moment* and my many other pursuits and projects.

I could not have told the stories of these women without the scholars and writers who trod this ground before me, in particular those who contributed to the Jewish Women Archives (JWA), a magnificent online endeavor.

One last note: I want to remember and honor all the many trailblazing women who deserved to be in this book but could not be included because of time and space. I hope readers who like what they have read here will go on to learn more about other remarkable women.

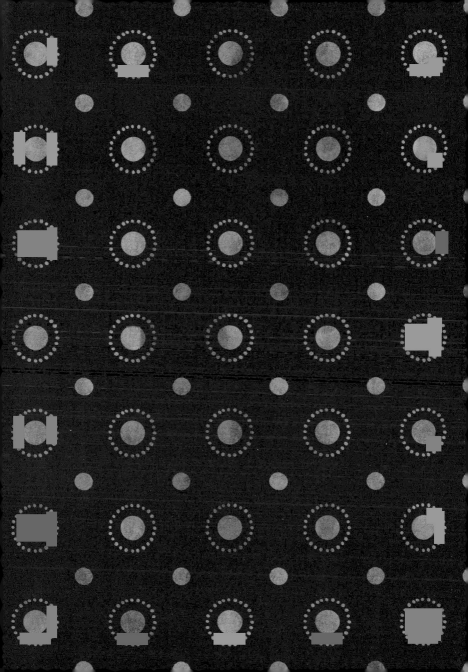

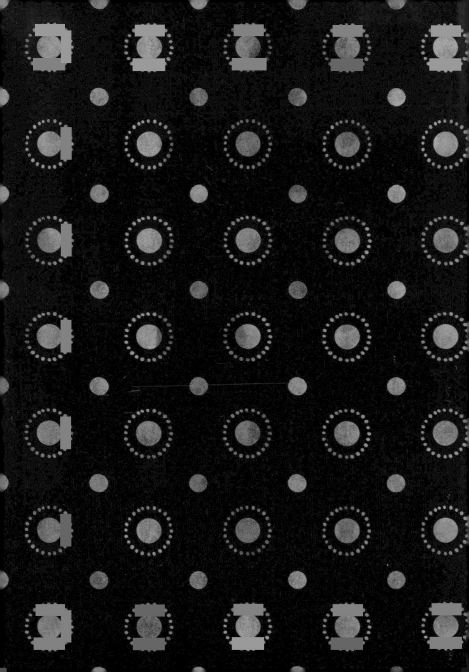

CAROL GUZY

ABOUT THE AUTHOR

Nadine Epstein is an award-winning journalist and writer.
She is editor-in-chief and CEO of *Moment Magazine*
(momentmag.com). Cofounded by the late Nobel Peace
Prize recipient Elie Weisel and the late Leonard Fein, the
magazine is dedicated to providing readers with enlight-
ening, lively, and differing perspectives on contemporary
Jewish religious, political, and cultural issues. As the
founder and director of the Center for Creative Change,
she has launched projects from the Daniel Pearl Inves-
tigative Journalism Initiative to help young reporters
expose prejudice to the publishing imprint Moment-
Books. Her most recent venture, the Role Model Project

(momentmag.com/role-model-project), is designed to help young people identify inspirational role models. It was established in memory of her dear friend Justice Ruth Bader Ginsburg.

An award-winning journalist with limitless curiosity, she considers herself incredibly lucky to have fashioned a career that allows her to research, write, and edit articles and books about whatever interests her, and gives her the opportunity to speak with and learn from the most thoughtful and inventive people of our time. Her confidence in the power of human creativity is paired with her beliefs that greatly expanding the number of women in major leadership positions will make the world a better place for all, and that by working together, we will overcome prejudice of all kinds. She speaks and leads conversations about these and other topics worldwide.

Nadine is also a visual artist whose work has been featured in newspapers, magazines, galleries, and museums. She lives in Washington, DC, with her family and invites you to visit her website

NADINEEPSTEIN.COM
@NADINEEPSTEINDC

ABOUT THE ILLUSTRATOR

Bee Johnson is an illustrator living and working in Queens, New York. Her illustrations have appeared in publications such as *The New York Times*, *National Geographic*, and *The Washington Post*.

As the mother of two young daughters and a long-time admirer of the late Justice Ruth Bader Ginsburg, she took special pleasure in illustrating the many women of purpose and strength in this book. You can visit her online.

BEEJOHNSON.COM
@BEEJOHNSONILLO